SEMIOTEXT(E) INTERVENTION SERIES

Published by Semiotext(e)
2007 Wilshire Blvd., Suite 427, Los Angeles, CA 90057
www.semiotexte.com

Thanks to Erik Morse.
The translator wishes to thank Susanna Proietti for her
invaluable help.

Design: Hedi El Kholti

ISBN: 978-1-58435-102-3
Distributed by The MIT Press, Cambridge, Mass.
and London, England
Printed in the United States of America
10 9 8 7 6 5 4 3 2

Christian Marazzi

The Violence of
Financial Capitalism

Translated by Kristina Lebedeva

and Jason Francis Mc Gimsey

semiotext(e)
intervention
series □ 2

Contents

It's not a question of worrying or of hoping for the best, but of finding new weapons.

— Gilles Deleuze

Introduction

VIOLENT FINANCE

The ball began in June 2007, when it became known that two hedge funds, managed by Bear Stearns, had invested in assets guaranteed by subprime loans and needed to put $3.8 billion of obligations up for sale. Within one minute, literally, one of the most important investment banks on Wall Street was compelled to sell itself to JP Morgan Chase at defeating prices, $2 per share, when only 48 hours before it cost $30.

A year later, with the bankruptcies of Washington Mutual, Wachovia, Fannie Mae, Freddie Mac, AIG, and Lehman Brothers, and then Citigroup, Bank of America, Northern Rock, UBS, Bank of Scotland, and many other financial institutions, one began to understand that the collapse of Lehman Brothers was not, in fact, an isolated episode and that the entire banking system was in one of the greatest crises of history. Already in December 2007, the central banks of five currency areas announced coordinated actions to sustain private banks. In January 2008, the Central European Bank, the Federal Reserve and the national Swiss Bank made additional financing operations. Since then there has been an impressive succession of interventions to rescue the banking and financial system. The last one (March 2009), taken by the Obama Administration was immediately judged as an nth degree fiasco by the winner of the Nobel prize in economics, Paul Krugman.

The abyss opened by derivative financial products seemed incommensurable. Public deficits increased within a few months to the levels of the Second World War, the geopolitical scenarios were being modified as needed and the crisis, instead of subduing, was inexorably expanding with its most devastating effects on employment, wages, and retirement. On the real lives of entire populations.

It is the crisis of crises, a crisis that has a long story and, in all likelihood, a long future. It is a violent crisis, of a violent finance, a crisis that witnessed the greats of the world economy (G20) meeting in London, April 2, concerned with reviving the global economy by actions of intervention that only partially reflected the gravity of the problems accumulated through years of the financialization of the economy. It is a systemic crisis that saw an entire economic, political, and cultural model collapse under the pressure of its own contradictions, a crisis in which anger, disenchantment, distrust, and protest are limited to questioning the very limits of capitalism.

1

THE BECOMING OF THE CRISIS

Before interpreting the crisis of financial capitalism, it may be useful to summarize some facts about the macro-economic and global financial situation that has emerged over the last year as a result of the real estate and banking bubble. Let us say from the outset, citing an article by Martin Wolf, an intelligent supporter of liberal globalization in the *Financial Times* (January 7, 2009), that, although necessary, the dramatic increase of the American federal deficit and the expansion of credit from central banks all over the world will have *temporary effects* but will not be able to restore normal and lasting rates of development. It is thus possible that over the course of 2009 and beyond, we will witness the succession of a false recovery, a hiccuping movement in the stock exchange followed by repetitive down-turns and subsequent interventions of governments attempting to contain the crisis. In short, we are confronted by a systemic crisis requiring "radical changes" that, at least for the time being, no one can really prescribe in a convincing manner. Monetary policy, even if it has some efficacy in improving economies during recessions, is entirely ineffective when it enters into a depressive crisis like the one we are experiencing. The reason is that in a crisis like the present one (*The Economist* called it "the biggest bubble in history"), which in some sense resembles what Japan experienced in the 1990s, the transmission channels of monetary interventions (reduction of interest rate, insertion of liquidity, interventions in the exchange rate, increase in the banking reserve funds) are irrelevant. That is, they cannot transmit the credit impulses to companies and domestic economies necessary to revive consumption. The difference being that, in the case of Japan, the bubble burst had depressive effects on investments in capital, which up until the 1980s represented 17% of Gross Domestic Product, while the crisis that broke out in the United States had direct effects on 70% of GDP resulting from the consumption in the domestic American economies. Given that "the US consumer is by far the most important consumer in the world, the global implications of America's post-bubble shake-out are likely to be far more severe than those Japan was subjected to" (Stephen Roach, "US Not Certain of Avoiding Japan-Style 'Lost Decade,'" *Financial Times*, January 14, 2009).

On the basis of a study by Carmen Reinhart from Maryland University and Kenneth Rogoff from Harvard ("The Aftermath of Financial Crises," December 2008, http://www.economics.harvard.edu/

faculty/rogofff/files/Aftermath.pdf), we see in what way this crisis is by far the deepest in the past few decades. Banking crises like this one, as the authors note in retrospect, last at least two years with severe drops in GDP. The collapses in the stock markets are profound, with an average fall in real prices of real estate assets of 35% over the span of 6 years and a 55% decline in prices of non-real estate assets over 3–4 years. The average unemployment rate rises by 7% in 4 years, while the output decreases by 9%. Moreover, the real value of public debt increases, on average, by 86% and this is only in small part due to the cost of bank recapitalization. Instead, it largely depends on the collapse of tax revenues.

An important difference between this crisis and the ones in the recent past is that the present one is a *global* crisis and not regional, like the others. As long as the rest of the world is in the position of being able to finance the US, like in the past, we can anticipate a containment of the crisis on a regional scale. This is because the American government can take advantage of a vast program of tax and monetary stimuli financed by the countries in surplus of saving from the purchase of American Treasury bills. But who today can help the US in the long run? The present difficulty consists in the fact that, being global, the crisis broke the very force that allowed the global economy to grow, albeit in an unequal way, over the last decades, i.e., the flux of demand from countries in the structural deficit of production (like the US) to countries with structural surplus (like China, Japan, Germany). However, when private spending collapses on a global scale, the efforts to increase the American demand no longer suffice. That is to say, actions to revive the demand on a global scale are required, even in the emerging countries with a surplus of production. At the moment, it does not seem that emerging countries can compensate for the loss of the internal demand of developed countries (so-called *decoupling*), since the crisis has particularly severe depressive effects for them as well. Nonetheless, according to the estimate of the World Bank, it cannot be excluded that, at least in the medium term (2010–2015) and with important differences between China, India, Russia, and South American countries, growth rates will continue to be maintained at an average of 4–5%. This possibility depends on the fact that of the total exports in the emerging countries (which averaged 35% of GDP in the emerging countries over the last 5 years), only 20% are exports to the developed countries, while 15% results from internal exchanges between emerging countries ("Emerging Markets: Stumble or Fall?" *The Economist*, January 10, 2009). In any case, in order to be able to pull the load of world demand, emerging countries must—besides raising internal wages—channel their savings no longer towards the Western countries in deficit, but towards internal demand, which robs the global monetary and financial circuit of the same mechanism that allowed the global economy to function despite, or even because of, profound structural imbalances. It is thus possible that, *after the crisis*, emerging countries will become the hegemonic economic force in which the savings of the developed countries will be invested, thereby inverting flows of capital and somewhat reducing the level of consumption in developed countries. But no one can foresee the *duration* of this crisis and, therefore, the political, in addition to economic, capacity to manage the cumulative multiplication of social and political contradictions that are already manifesting themselves is essential.

Thus we cannot but focus our attention on the trend of demand in advanced decifit countries, particularly the US. If we take into account that, in the US, between the third quarter of 2007 and the third quarter of 2008, there was a fall in demand in private credit of 13%, it is certain that the net savings are destined to remain positive for several years—and not just in the US. In other words, private citizens will do everything possible to reduce their private debts, which can only annul the monetary actions for the revival of private consumption. Assuming for a moment a financial surplus (that is, lack of consumption) in the private sector of 6% of the GDP and a structural deficit in the commercial balance of 4%

of the GDP, the tax deficit necessary to compensate for the reduction of internal and external demand would have to be, according to Wolf's estimate in the cited article, equal to 10% of the GDP—"*indefinitely*"! Reducing public debt of such a scale, "in a reasonable time span," entails enormous efforts, especially if we take into account that today the federal American deficit is already around 12% of the GDP—at the levels of the Second World War.

As if this were not enough, we should not forget the obstacles to debt redemption for companies caused by nominal interest rates tending to zero and the reduction of prices (deflation): in situations of this kind, real interest rates are very high and debt repayment consequently becomes quite costly. It is precisely for this reason that a second wave of banking crises cannot be excluded. As Michel Aglietta writes, "If such is the situation, the banks are risking a second financial shock—return shock, the shock of insolvent company debt. This is how an economic depression can propagate itself through reciprocal reinforcement of debt redemption in finance and economic deflation" (*La crise. Pourquoi en est-on arrivé là? Comment en sortir?*, Michalon, Parigi, 2008, p. 118).

According to Paul Krugman, the $825 billion economic stimulus program proposed by Obama (reduced by Congress and the Senate, on February 11, to $789.5 billion) is not even remotely sufficient to fill the "output gap" between the potential growth and effective GDP growth in times of crisis: "Given sufficient demand for its output, America would produce more than $30 trillion worth of goods and services over the next two years. But with both consumer spending and business investment plunging, a huge gap is opening up between what the American economy can produce and what it's able to sell. And the Obama plan is nowhere near big enough to fill this 'output gap.'" Now, Krugman wonders, why is Obama not trying to do more? Certainly, there are dangers tied to the government loan on a vast scale, but the consequences of inadequate action are not much better than sliding into a prolonged deflationary trap of the Japanese kind, an inevitable spiral if the actions of intervention are not adequate (i.e., around $2.1 trillion). Or, Krugman still wonders, is it the lack of spending opportunities that limits his plan? "There are only a limited number of 'shovel-ready' public investment projects—that is, projects that can be started quickly enough to help the economy in the near term. But there are other forms of public spending, especially on health care, that could do good while aiding the economy in its hour of need." Yet again, is there an element of political prudence behind Obama's decision, i.e., the attempt to remain under a trillion dollars for the economic plan's final cost to ensure the support of Republicans? ("The Obama Gap," *The New York Times*, January 9, 2009).

Obama's plan is composed of 60% public spending (health care, investments in infrastructure and education, aids to homeowners risking foreclosure) and 35% tax reductions. Joseph Stiglitz, in his interview in the *Financial Times* ("Do not Squander America's Stimulus on Tax Cut," 16 January, 2009) has, however, urged the US not to squander the stimulus on tax breaks, which, in this crisis, are doomed to fail. For example, only 50% of the tax cut that came into effect in February 2008 increased spending, while the remaining part of the increase in available income was used to reduce private debts. Today, a tax break would most likely be used almost exclusively to reduce debts, except perhaps in the case of poor families with a high tendency to consumption. It would be much better, if one indeed wants to persist on the path of tax cuts, to limit the breaks for companies to increases in investments, preferably if they are innovative. "Spending on infrastructure, education and technology create assets; they increase future productivity" (Stiglitz).

Independently of the fact that state stimuli result mainly from increases in discretionary expenditures, like in the US, or by the more or less automatic effects of an increase in social spending, like in Europe, state governance of the crisis depends in the last analysis on the capacity to borrow capital from the bond market. The dimension of the issuance of public bonds scheduled for 2009 is stratospheric: it goes from an estimated $2.2 or maybe $2.5 billion in the US, or 14% of the GDP, to $215 billion worth of bonds sold in England (10% of the GDP), to issuances of significant amounts of bonds in every country of the world, including Germany, which at first tried to resist tax stimuli of the Anglo-Saxon kind (initially accused of "crass Keynesianism" by chancellor Merkel).

The recourse to bond markets by the US in order to collect capital to cover the growing deficit should not, in principle, pose a particular problem, especially in deflationary periods like the one we are going through, characterized by continuous reductions in interest rates (which for investors in bonds means real fixed and relatively high earnings).

Nonetheless, the expectation of a collapse in market inflation and, consequently, a possible increase in state difficulties in honoring debt with growing tax revenues (normally caused by inflation), is already causing an increase in real tax interest rates on T-bills, and this is also the case in the economically wealthiest countries. In fact, international investors in public bonds demand substantially higher nominal and real earnings in order to better protect themselves against the risks of state defaults. According to the analysts, as much as there are signals of an economic bubble on the markets that can explain the distortion of prices, "it is nonetheless somewhat unsettling that real interest rates have risen as governments started to borrow" (Chris

Giles, David Oakley, and Michael Mackenzie, "Onerous issuance," *Financial Times*, January 7, 2009; see also Steve Johnson, "Inflation Fears to Hit Debt Auction," *FT Weekly Review of the Fund Management Industry*, March 30, 2009). For countries like Spain, Portugal, Greece, Ireland, and Italy, whose differential earnings in T-bills had been a little higher than those of Germany until 2007, the problems with financing public deficits have been increasing in an obvious way since December 2008.

Alfonso Tuor has summarized the consequences of the crisis of the public debt on a world scale as follows: "the short-term consequence of these policies is a crisis of trust in bonds with which states finance the public debt. There is no lack of premonitory signals: the last in chronological order came from Great Britain, where, for the first time over the last seven years an auction of public bonds failed, despite the decision of the Bank of England to purchase them for more than 100 billion euros. The crisis in public debt is destined to provoke a subsequent escalation of interventions in the central banks. The latter would be called upon to buy them in large quantities and to print more currency. With what consequences? Strong inflation, if there is the interlude of a short recovery, or, in some countries (the top candidates being Great Britain and the US), currency crises and hyperinflation. Which, for the citizen, means an impressive destruction of private and retirement savings, but for the financial oligarchy an ideal instrument to destroy the value of the enormous quantity of toxic activities held by the large banks" ("Chi pagherà il conto della crisi?," Corriere del Ticino, March 27, 2009).

Despite the ten years of the euro, the markets are working with precise distinctions between the risk countries within this very eurozone—a problem not easily resolvable by the recourse to the creation of a currency by member countries or by issuing union-bonds, which would damage the strong countries in the eurozone. This again urgently raises the question of a real unification of state policies, particularly the social ones, within the EU.

In this phase, with few investors disposed to purchase public obligations in the face of an extremely high offer to issue public bonds, the risk of crowding out (of leaving the private bond market) is entirely real. Competition in bond markets between private companies and governments risks further inhibiting the overcoming of the crisis, to the extent that, for the companies involved, the issuance of bonds can become particularly costly. At this point, the State—as is already happening in the US with the support of automobile companies—can be compelled to directly support private companies by purchasing their bonds, which would mean the beginning of a process of quasi-nationalization (without, however, the right to vote from the stockholder State) of non-financial companies. This process would follow the one that began in the banking and financial sector with the interventions of central banks in the last months. If then, as a hypothesis, the world economy were to start up again, the inverse process of crowding out, i.e., the withdrawal of public bonds towards the private ones, would significantly increase debt service in all indebted countries.

"The hopes of overcoming the crisis," writes Alfonso Tuor, "are melting like the snow under the sun. A series of negative events are curbing even the most incurable optimists and forcing stock to go below the lowest levels, registered in the course of November" ("Crisi dell'Est, nuovo incubo dell'Europa," *Corriere del Ticino*, February 19, 2009). The crisis of the former Soviet bloc countries, which in the last years have been indebted to the European banks in Swiss francs, American dollars, Japanese yen, Swedish crowns, and Euro—in order to compensate for the scarcity of internal savings and to reinforce the expansion of credit to small and medium companies, the expansion of mortgage credit to low interest rates and real estate overinvestments—seriously risks boomeranging against the European banks. The latter, particularly the Austrian, Italian, and Swedish banks, have acquired significant shareholdings (up to 80%) in Hungarian, Slovenian, and Slovak banks, which means that an insolvency crisis in the domestic East European economies—a crisis entirely similar to those in Mexico,

Argentina, or Southeast Asia, a kind of European subprime crisis—immediately becomes a problem of the European Union, in addition to that of its banks. "The crisis started in the US, but Europe is where it might turn into catastrophe," writes Wolfgang Münchau ("Eastern Crisis That Could Wreck the Eurozone," *Financial Times*, February 23, 2009). In this case, an intervention to support Eastern economies, like, for example, an intervention of the International Monetary Fund, to escape a contagious crisis of payment balances due to a chain of devaluations of local currencies, seems entirely inefficient. "If the exchange rates," wonders Münchau, "were to drop even further, the failures of domestic economies could increase dramatically. Are we, Europeans, ready to help them?" It is difficult to imagine European citizens running to help the mythic Polish plumber. The split at the heart of Europe due to the collapse of the former communist Soviet bloc seriously risks calling into question the very future of the EU ("The Bill That Could Break up Europe," *The Economist*, February 28, 2009).

The scenario at the forefront here is a massive and continuous increase in unemployment on a worldwide scale and a generalized reduction in incomes and rent, in the face of a vertiginous increase in a comprehensive tax deficit. The financial crisis is having devastating effects on the manufacturing industry and world commerce, with millions of dismissals, closedowns of thousands of factories and biblical returns of immigrants to their countries of origin ("The Collapse of Manufacturing," *The Economist*, February 21, 2009). For the moment, that is, beginning from the crisis of Bear Stearns, proceeding to the crisis of the Lehman Brothers, American International Group and Citigroup, the "socialist turn" of liberal governments to sustain the banking, financial and insurance systems by means of recapitalization and monetary issuances does not seem to be able to avoid chain bankruptcy of all insolvent decentralized banks due to an improbable quantity of toxic assets. "It would take another $1.4 trillion," writes the economist Nouriel Roubini from New York University, "to bring back the capital of banks to the level they had before the crisis; and such massive additional recapitalization is needed to resolve the credit crunch and restore lending to the private sector. So these figures suggest that the US banking system is effectively insolvent in the aggregate; most of the UK banking system looks insolvent too; and many other banks in continental Europe are also insolvent" ("It Is Time to Nationalize Insolvent Banking Systems," *http://www.roubini.com /roubini-monitor/255507*, February 10, 2009). There is no sufficient private capital to absorb the present and foreseeable losses and reconstruct bank assets. The resources for this must be public (whether one likes it or not). The slowness in recognizing that it is a question, no more and no less, of an insolvency crisis of the banking system as a whole, will involve extremely high prices. The same is true for the difficulty untangling the complex knot of the nationalization of the major banks (even on the day when the American State becomes the principal shareholder of the colossal Citigroup with 36% of capital stock).

It is entirely likely that in two years the economies of all countries, despite the actions of the economic stimulus, will still be in depression (stag deflation), just as it is possible that each country will try to reintroduce in their native land the quotas of demand by means of devaluations and protectionist actions (deglobalization) in order to try to postpone as much as possible the confrontation with taxpayers called on to pay public deficits. The margins of economic and monetary policy to effectively manage the crisis are extremely restricted. Classical Keynesian actions lack transmission channels of state stimuli to the real economy, to the demand of goods and services, and investment goods. On the other hand, it makes little sense to speak of a new Bretton Woods without taking into account the profound transformations in the international monetary arrangement, the transformations that reflect the crisis of national sovereignty resulting from globalization. If one instead wants to speak of a New Deal, i.e., of a process of supporting incomes, employment, and credit system at the "grassroots" level, it will then be necessary to analyze social forces, subjects, and forms of struggle that can substantiate in a politically innovative way an escape route from this crisis.

2

FINANCIAL LOGICS

The process of financialization that led to the crisis we are living in now is distinct from all other phases of financialization historically recorded in the twentieth century. Classical financial crises were situated at a precise moment of the economic cycle, particularly at the end of the cycle, in conjunction with a fall of profit margins as a result of capitalist competition on an international scale, in addition to social forces undermining geopolitical equilibrium in the international division of labor. Typical twentieth-century financialization thus represented an attempt, somewhat "parasitic" and "desperate," to recover what capital could no longer get in the real economy in financial markets. As Charles P. Kindleberger, the greatest historian of finance, showed, ever since the 17th century financial cycles have always been constituted by a precise sequence: a phase of impetus, one of collective infatuation and overtrading of stock markets, a phase of fear and disorder, followed by a phase of consolidation, and, finally, a phase of reorganization. "In the phase of overtrading, activity becomes frenetic, the aspirations of individuals do not cease to grow, the velocity of transactions is accelerated and the prices of real or virtual financial assets—that is, the price of elements constitutive of people's wealth—are inflamed" (M. Aglietta, *op. cit.*, p. 8). The accumulation and specific centralization of the "interest-bearing capital" as Marx defines it in Volume III of *Capital*, also called "fictitious capital" managed primarily by banks with autonomous production of money by means of money, indeed epitomized one of the salient characteristics of twentieth century financialization processes (having already been pointed out by Marx in the second half of the nineteenth century). Financial crises were thus based on a contradictory relationship between real and financial economies, a relationship that today is no longer expressed in the same terms.

The financial economy today is pervasive, that is, it spreads across the entire economic cycle, co-existing with it, so to speak, from start to finish. Figuratively speaking, finance is present even when you go shopping at the supermarket and use your credit card. The automobile industry, to give only one example, functions entirely upon credit mechanisms (installments, leasing, etc.), so that the problems of a General Motors have just as much to do with the production of cars as, if not above all, with the weakness of GMAC, its branch specializing in consumer credit, indispensable for selling their products to consumers. This means that we are in a historical period

in which finance is *cosubstantial* with the very production of goods and services.

In addition to industrial profits not reinvested in
instrumental capital and in wages, the sources fueling
today's financialization have multiplied: there are
profits deriving from the returns of dividends and
royalties from offshore investments; flows of interest
coming from Third World debt to which flows of
interest on international bank loans to emerging countries are added; flows of interest on international bank
loans to the emerging countries; surplus-values derived
from raw materials; the sums accumulated by individuals and wealthy families invested in stock markets,
retirement and investment funds. The multiplication
and extension of the sources and agents of "interest-
bearing capital" are, without a doubt, one of the
distinctive, unforeseen and problematic traits of
this new financial capitalism, especially if we reflect
upon the possibility or impossibility of modifying
this system, of "re-financing" it, reestablishing a
"more balanced" relation between the real and
financial economies.

Like its predecessors, this financialization also
begins from a block of accumulation understood as
non-reinvestment of profits in directly productive
processes (constant capital, i.e., instrumental goods
and variable capital, i.e., wages). In fact, it began with
the crisis of growth of Fordist capitalism in the
1970s. In those years, there were all the premises of

a repetition of classical financialization based on the dichotomy between real (industrial) and monetary economies, with the consequent shifting of profit quotas to financial markets to ensure profitable growth without accumulation. In the beginning of the 1980s, "the primary source of financial bubbles was the trend of growth of non-accumulated profit, the growth caused by a double movement: on the one hand, a generalized decrease in wages and, on the other hand, the stagnation—i.e., decrease—of the rate of accumulation despite the reestablishment of profit rate" (Michel Husson, "Les enjeux de la crise," *La Brèche*, November 2008). By accumulation rate, the net growth of the amount of net capital is intended, while profit rate means the relationship between profits and capital: the divergence between the two rates starting from 1980 represents one of the many sure indications of financialization. But, other sources of "accumulation" of financial capital are gradually added to the nonreinvested industrial profits, a fact to keep in mind in order to understand the transformations of the post-Fordist model of crisis-development. In particular, financialization involved a process of banking de-mediation regarding the financialization of economic growth (the predominance of the Anglo-Saxon model over the Rhenish one), but also involved a process of the *multiplication* of financial intermediaries resulting from the deregulation and liberalization of the economy.

The transition from the Fordist mode of production to "stock managerial capitalism," which is at the basis of today's financial capitalism, is in fact explained by the drop in profits (around 50%) between the 1960s and the 1970s due to the exhaustion of the technological and economic foundations of Fordism, particularly by market saturation of mass consumption goods, the rigidity of productive processes, constant capital and the politically "downwardly rigid" working wage. At the height of its development, in a specific organic composition of capital (i.e., the relationship between constant and variable capital), Fordist capitalism was no longer able to "suck" surplus-value from working-class living labor. "Hence, from the second half of the 1970s on, the primary propulsive force of the world economy was the endless attempt of capitalist companies—under the demands of their owners and investors—to bring the profit rate back up, using various techniques, to the highest levels of twenty years before" (Luciano Gallino, *L'impresa irresponsabile*, Einaudi, Torino, 2005). We know how it went: reduction in the cost of labor, attacks on unions, automatization and robotization of entire labor processes, delocalization to countries with low wages, precarization of labor and diversification of consumption models. And, of course, financialization, i.e., profit increases not as excess from sales over costs (that is, not in accordance with manufacturing-Fordist logic) but as excess value in the stock market "at the time T2 with respect to T1—where the gap between T1 and T2 can be a few days."

In fact, the recourse to financial markets on the part of companies in order to reestablish profit margin has never had anything to do with financing company activities by issuing new bonds—this is because companies have always had wide margins of self-financing. American companies, the companies in the largest shareholding country in the world, have used financing by the issuances of assets to supply only 1% of their needs; German companies only 2%. In other words, the financialization of the economy has been a process of recovering capital's profitability after the period of profit margin decreases, an apparatus to enhance capital's profitability *outside* immediately productive processes. It is this very apparatus that led companies to internalize in an "irresponsible" way the paradigm of shareholder value, the primacy of shareholder value over that of the multiplicity of "interest bearers"—the latter being called stakeholder value (wage earners, consumers, suppliers, the environment, future generations). The (industrial) profit quota of the total income of companies, which in the 1960s and 1970s had gone from 24% to 15–17% in the US, has never since exceeded 14–15% and financialization is structured accordingly, becoming for all intents and purposes the modus operandi of contemporary capitalism.

"As Greta Krippner has shown on the basis of a thorough analysis of the available evidence, not only had the share of total US corporate profits accounted for by finance, insurance, and real estate (FIRE) in the 1980s nearly caught up with and, in 1990, ~~supposed~~ *surpassed* the share accounted for by manufacturing; more important, in the 1970s and 1980s, *non-financial firms themselves* sharply increased their investment in financial assets relative to that in plants and equipment, and became increasingly dependent on financial sources of revenue and profit relative to that earned from productive activities. Particularly significant is Krippner's finding that manufacturing not only dominates but *leads* this trend towards the 'financialization' of the non-financial economy" (Giovanni Arrighi, *Adam Smith in Beijing : lineages of the twenty-first century*, Verso, 2007, pp. 140). This is enough to definitively discard the distinction between (industrial) real and financial economies, distinguishing industrial profits from "fictitious" financial ones. As well as to stop identifying, from either a theoretical or historical point of view, capitalism with industrial capitalism (as Arrighi writes, a typical act of faith of orthodox Marxism that does not merit a justification). If one really wants to speak of "irresponsible companies" to describe the paradigm of shareholder value—adopted by companies over the last thirty years—one would do well to speak of the transformation of the production process based on the "profits becoming rent," to use Carlo Vercellone's apt expression ("The Crisis of the

Law of Value and the Becoming-Rent of Profit,"
in *Crisis in the Global Economy, Financial Markets, Social Struggles, and New Political Scenarios*, ed. by Andrea Fumagali and Sandro Mezzandra, Semiotext(e), 2010).

There is no doubt that, in the post-Fordist config-uration of financial capitalism, where the role of wages is reduced and precarized and investements in capital stagnate, the problem of the *realization* of profits (that is, selling the surplus-value product) remains the role of consumption by means of *non-wage incomes*. Under this *distributive* profile, the reproduction of capital (characterized by the extremely high polarization of wealth) is carried out partly thanks to the increase in the consumption of rentiers and partly thanks to the indebted consumption of wage earners. Financialization has redistributed, although in a strongly unequal and precarious way (think about retirement rent derived from integrated retirement funds in accordance with the primacy of contributions), financial rent to wage workers in the double form of non-real-estate and real estate incomes (in the US, 20% and 89% respectively). There is thus a kind of becoming-rent of salary in addition to the becoming-rent of profit.

The indebtedness of domestic economies, to which a more or less pronounced reduction of savings according to whether one is in the US or Europe corresponds, is what allowed financial capitalism to reproduce itself on an enlarged and global scale. It is possible to affirm that, parallel to the reduction of the redistributive function of the social state, it is now assisted by a kind of privatization of deficit spending à la Keynes, i.e., the creation of an additional demand by means of private debt (with a relative displacement of wealth toward private domestic economies).

American mortgage indebtedness, which reached more than 70% of the GDP with a total indebtedness of domestic economies equaling 93% of the GDP, constituted the primary source of increase in consumption since 2000 and, beginning in 2002, the driving force of the real estate bubble. Consumption was fueled by so-called remortgaging, the possibility of renegotiating mortgage loans in order to get new credit, thanks to the inflationary increase in house prices. This mechanism, called home equity extraction, played a fundamental role in the American economic growth. The US Bureau of Economic Analysis estimated that the gains from GDP growth due to the increase in home equity extraction were, on average, 1.5% between 2002 and 2007. Without the positive impact of mortgage credit and the subsequent increase in consumption, the growth of the American GDP would be equal to, or outright less than, that of the eurozone (Jacques Sapir, *L'économie politique internationale de la crise et la question du "nouveau Bretton Woods": Leçons pour des temps de crise, Mimeo*, sapir@msh-paris.fr).

The explosion of private indebtedness was facilitated, especially after the collapse of Nasdaq in 2000–2002, by a very expansive monetary policy and banking deregulation, a policy that reinforced the securitization of debt-based obligations: Collaterized Debt Obligation and Collaterized Loan Obligations, to which are added Credit Default Swaps, derivative insurance obligations that are swapped (in fact, bartered) between operators in order to protect themselves against investment risks. The total of all these credit derivatives amounts to something like $62 trillion, a multiplication of 100 in ten years (for a description of securitized bonds and other financial instruments, see the brief dictionary in the Appendix).

Securitization allows the loans supplied to clients to be cleaned from the fiscal balances of institutions or credit agencies (mortgage, but also credit card) by selling them to investment banks. The latter constitutes a credit pool with differentiated risks (from good to less good) and, on this basis, issue assets which are then ceded to financial structures created *ad hoc* (called conduits and special vehicles) that finance the purchase price through short term debts. Finally, bonds are placed with investors as hedge funds, investment banks, retirement and investment funds. In such a way, someone's mortgage debts become a high-paying business (as long as it lasts) in someone else's hands.

"In order to describe this mechanism, the expression *originate-to-distribute* is used. As in an assembly line, various specialized firms coordinate their shares in order to fabricate, assemble, and synthesize investment products starting with aggregates of real estate credits. The actors in this assembly line are brokers of real estate loans, directly in contact with consumers, the intermediaries who buy wholesale and bring together credit aggregates in accordance with the specifications of financial institutions and hedge funds that, at the end of the line, provide capital, and, finally rating agencies that determine whether the composition of these asset portfolios satisfies their criteria of quality" (Martha Poon, "Aux origines était la bulle. La mécanique des fluides des subprimes," http://www.mouvements.info/spip.php?article379).

The complex financial engineering substantially allows for the artificial increase of the total amount of credit (leverage effect), cleaning the balances of credit institutions from loans as to enable them to provide new loans. It is a kind of multiplication of the breads because a split between bond flows *qua* right to a part of created profit and of purely monetary interest and dividend flows is inherent in the multiplication of credit by means of securitization.

There is no doubt that derivative obligations created on subprime mortgage credits immediately became the scapegoat of the global financial crisis, earning the name of "toxic" assets. The securitization of subprime loans is, in fact, situated at the center of the transformations of the world of American mortgage finance where the industry of real estate loans is articulated by the wider market of investment products based on active capital (asset backed securities). In the latter, all the evils of the new finance are condensed: laxist practices of credit, rushing to search for easy money from bonds issued on loans, nonchalantly supplying loans to financially untrustworthy people, the violation of rules, naiveté in calculating risks, fraud, etc.

As Martha Poon reminds us in the article we just cited, "the system of exchanging real estate credits is not a novelty in the US, since it goes back to the New Deal. But in the recent period, there has been a shift of this traditionally circumscribed practice into a market whose liquidity was sustained by organisms guaranteed by the state—government-sponsored enterprises or GSE, better known as Freddie Mac and Fannie Mae—and by specialized lenders whose activity was financed by deposits in an industry largely sustained by investments in risk-capital." So much that in the GSE the only securitized loans were the prime loans, while the subprime loans were by definition excluded (on the creation, in 1971, of the prime derivative obligation, called "Ginnie Mae," see my book *E il denaro va. Esodo e revoluzione dei mercati finanziari*, Bollati Boringhieri/Edizioni Casagrande, Torino-Bellinzona, 1998, pp. 65–69).

"The financial crisis," writes Paul Krugman, "has, inevitably, led to a hunt for villains. Some of the accusations are entirely spurious, like the claim, popular on the right, that all our problems were caused by the Community Reinvestment Act, which supposedly forced banks to lend to minority home buyers who then defaulted on their mortgages; in fact the act was passed in 1977, which makes it hard to see how it can be blamed for a crisis that didn't happen until three decades later. Anyway, the act applied only to depository banks, which accounted for a small fraction of the bad loans during the housing bubble" (*The Return of Depression Economics and the Crisis of 2008*, W. W. Norton & Company, 2009, p 162).

Moreover, it may be useful to recall that the securitization of prime loans in the course of the 1970s and 1980s has facilitated the expansion of not only the American middle class. "During the years of inflation, Americans, Canadians, Japanese and a large part of Europe underwent the fascination with owning a house. House prices went up until they had no relationship with the purchase price and everyone was satisfied. Satisfied at least while the abundance lasted, especially if the property cost quite a lot. The inflation of the value of houses was in fact a powerful mechanism of wealth redistribution. Whoever did not own a house was at a disadvantage: they continued to pay for evermore expensive goods and services like everyone else but, in contrast to home owners, were not compensated by tax-exempt gains in capital" (Marco d'Eramo, *Il maiale e il*

grattacielo. Chicago: una storia del nostro futuro,
Feltrinelli, Milano, 1995, p. 39).

Beginning with the 2000–2002 crisis of the new
economy, the American real estate market witnessed
a spectacular acceleration, especially if we recall that,
already in 2001, real estate prices were considerably
high; so high that analysts already took for granted
the existence of a bubble in the sector by 2002.
Instead, thanks to the securitization of subprime
loans, it was possible to postpone the inflation of the
real estate sector until the bubble burst in 2007.

The expansion of subprime loans shows that, in
order to raise and make profits, finance also needs to
involve the poor, in addition to the middle class. In
order to function, this capitalism must invest in the
bare life of people who cannot provide any guarantee,
who offer nothing apart from themselves. It is a capitalism that turns bare life into a direct source of
profit. It does so on the basis of a probability calculation according to which the lacking debt repayment
is considered "manageable," i.e., negligible, when
considered on the scale of the entire population. The
financial logic underlying the calculation of probability
is, in fact, particularly cynical: assets issued on the
basis of the mortgage credit pool and grouped together
by investment banks are created in accordance with
the principle of subordination, i.e., a hierarchy of risks
internal to the assets issued. The first lot, the lower
one, has a high risk. The intermediate one has a

reduced risk, and the highest one (super senior and senior), made up of the oldest, best assets, are considered particularly secure. The greater lot is thus *protected* by the lesser ones, in the sense that the latter will be the most exposed part of the securitized assets that will be the first to explode in the event of investor loss. The access to housing is created on the basis of mathematical models of risk where people's life means absolutely nothing, where the poor are "played" against the less poor, where the social right to housing is artificially subordinated to the private right to realize a profit. May the academic economists who all these years have been putting their scientific competence and their dignity at the disposal of financial industry find peace in their consciousness (on how today's financial crisis also reveals the crisis of academic economic science, see David Colander et al., "The Financial Crisis and the Systemic Failure of Academic Economics," http://economistsview.typepad.com /economistsview/2009/02/the-financial-crisis-and -the-systemic-failure-of-academic-economics.html).

Finance functions on the expectation of increasing and "infinite" growth in real estate prices (wealth effect), an inflationary increase without which it would be impossible to co-opt the potential have-nots—the necessary condition of ensuring the continuity of financial profits. It is a sort of Ponzi scheme or an airplane game in which those who came in last allow those who came in first to be remunerated. Something like St. Anthony's Chain, devised by the ex-president of Nasdaq, Bernard Madoff, that managed to collect something like $50 billion involving an impressive number of respectable financial operators and banks.

The threshold of this inclusive process is given in the contradiction between social ownership of a good (such as a house) and private ownership rights, between the expansion of social needs and the private logic of market financing. Social conflicts as well as capital's capacity or incapacity to overcome this crisis is at stake on this threshold. It is a question of a *temporal threshold*; think, for example, about the architecture of typical mortgage contracts on subprime loans. The formula of 2 + 28—where, in the first two years, mortgage interests are fixed and low, precisely for co-opting more and more "owners," and the other 28 years they are at variable rates, thus subjected to the general trend of conjuncture and of monetary policy—represents an example of the contradiction between social ownership rights and private property rights. After two years of relative use-value governance (the right to the access to housing), we move on to 28 years of exchange-value governance with extremely violent effects of expulsion/exclusion. In such a way, the financial logic produces a *common* (goods) that it then divides and privatizes through the expulsion of the "inhabitants of the common" by means of the artificial creation of *scarcity* of all kinds—scarcity of financial means, liquidity, rights, desire, and power. This is a process similar to seventeenth century enclosures where peasants—living on and off the land as a common good—were expunged by the processes of privatization and division of the common land, a process that gave rise to the modern proletariat and its bare life.

When Augusto Illuminati speaks of Spinoza and his resistance to the norm and the discipline of sovereignty, he highlights the decidedly juridical-normative nature of the processes of enclosures: Spinoza "does not ignore the land, but his campaign is not circumscribed by the eighteenth century enclosures, fenced in by farming and hunting, where the sheep—as the *Levellers* said—devoured men. It is not circumscribed by the land where men are reduced to inert sheep learning only to serve, because it is neither peace nor citizenship, but rather *solitude*, desert" (*Spinoza atlantico*, Edizioni Ghilbi, Milano, 2008, p. 15). Originary or primitive accumulation, as shown by Sandro Mezzandra, i.e., the salarization and proletarization of millions of people through the expulsion from their own land, is thus a process that historically reemerges every time the expansion of capital clashes with the common produced by social relations and cooperations free from the laws of capitalist exploitation (S. Mezzadra, "La 'cosiddetta' accumulazione originaria," in AAVV, *Lessico marxiano*, minifestolibri, Roma, 2008). The common produced by free social relations thus *precedes* the capitalist appropriation of that very common.

3

ON THE BECOMING-RENT OF PROFIT

The non-parasitic role of finance, its capacity to produce rent to ensure the increase in consumption, the
increase in effective demand necessary for GDP
growth, is, however, not only explained from a distributive point of view. It is very well true that
finance is nourished on non-accumulated profit not
reinvested in capital (constant and variable), and
exponentially multiplied thanks to financial engineering, just as it is true that the increase in profit
allows for the distribution of surplus-value quotas to
the holders of patrimonial shares. Under this profile
(*distributive*, let us repeat), the analysis of financialization and its intrinsic instability highlights real and
indeed perverse processes of autonomization of
financial capital from any collective interest (wage
and occupational stability, the collapse of retirement
rents and of savings invested in stock, the impossibility of accessing consumption in credit, the vapor-
ization of stocks in research). It highlights autoreferential dynamics where the search for ever-higher
shareholder earnings generates the increase of fictitious profits through the proliferation of financial

instruments—unmanageable because they are outside all rules and control.

The crisis-development in this mode of production thus acquires a discrepancy between social needs and financial logic based on criteria of hyper-profitability: in developed countries, the assertion of an anthropogenic model of "production of man by man" where consumption is increasingly oriented towards social, health, educational and cultural sectors, clashes with the privatization of many sectors previously managed by public criteria; in developing countries, the expansion of valorization provokes processes of hyper-exploitation and the destruction of local economies and the environment. The demands of profitability imposed by financial capitalism on the entire society reinforce social regression under the pressure of a growth model that, in order to distribute wealth, voluntarily sacrifices social cohesion and the quality of life itself. Wage deflation, pathologization of labor with increases in health costs generated by work stress (up to 3% of the GDP), worsening social balances and the irreparable deterioration of the environment are the effects of financial logic and of company delocalizations typical of global financial capitalism.

The *problem* is that, analyzed from a distributive point of view (*economistic* in the last instance), the crisis-development of financial capitalism leads to a veritable dead-end. As much as it is thrown out the window, the cliché that finance is parasitic implicitly comes back through the front door. The *impasse*, more theoretical than practico-political, is before everyone's eyes: the impossibility of elaborating strategies to overcome the crisis, the recourse to economic stimulus measures, on the one hand, presuppose the rescue of finance (of which we are really hostages), but, on the other hand, annul the very possibilities of economic revival.

Both the right and the left wish for an unlikely return to the real economy, veritable "re-industrializations" of the economy (preferably a little greener) in order to leave a finanzialized economy that is an accomplice to the destruction of income and employment. But no one worries anymore about describing the nature and functioning of the so-called "real economy." And thus they wish for state aid to industrial sectors suffering from overproduction, aid that is then translated into job and wage deductions, which certainly do not help (on the contrary) to revive the economy as a whole.

This urgency to return to "making things" is quite similar to the physiocratic critique of the supporters of the first industrial revolution; the idea that, unlike land products, "machines do not eat," forgetting that machines also help increase agricultural productivity too. It may be useful to stress that countries in commercial surplus, such as developing countries, but also Germany and Japan, were able to increase their exports essentially because the countries like the US and England, where the service sector—not just financial ones—is very developed, have ensured high growth rates of the *demand* of goods and services. And indeed, it is these very countries in commercial surplus that will greatly suffer the effects of the global crisis with the accumulation of enormous overproduction. The fact that the countries in surplus are the ones with the highest rates of savings certainly does not make things any simpler: it is true that a reduction of savings could increase internal demand, but this is exactly what will not happen for the simple reason that the saving will be used to confront the effects of the recession and the stagnation of employment and wages (Simon Tilford, "A Return to 'Making Things' is No Panacea," *Financial Times*, March 4, 2009).

This does not mean that the countries that have, in the last decades, greatly developed the services sector (certainly not just the US and Great Britain) should not redefine their own strategies of development on the basis of the crisis itself. But it is certain that it is not through a return to an ill-defined "real economy" that it will be possible to overcome the crisis. Countries in commercial deficit, for example, have very high rates of indebtedness in public and private sectors—an indebtedness, particularly the public one, destined to go up in this period of crisis—but they also have insufficient infrastructures resulting from years of disinvestment in the public sector.

Moreover, in these countries, there is a deficit of professional qualifications, a *deficit of valorization* of skills and diffused knowledges that damage, instead of help, knowledge workers.

The real blind spot, both theoretical and practical, has to do with the sterile distinction between the manufacturing sector (where things "are made") and the sector of immaterial activities, an opposition certainly reinforced by the abnormal development of the financial sector, but one that today risks damaging, in the name of "reindustrialization," all those creative, innovative activities with a high added value that have developed over these last few years. It is activities like these that should be most invested in.

Finally, as if that were not enough, both on the right and on the left, the nationalization of banks in insolvency is seen as inescapable and/or desirable, without questioning much the *social costs* of nationalization, especially when the latter are conceived as transitory actions with the future reprivatization of the same banks in mind. Toxic assets to the State, i.e., to the collectivity, good banks to private interests! This is the usual song and dance: socialize losses and privatize benefits (Matthew Richardson, "The Case For and Against Bank Nationalisation," http://www.voxeu.com/ index.php?q=node/3143).

In order to overcome this impasse, it is necessary to critically analyze the crisis of financial capitalism, which means starting from scratch, i.e., from that increase in profits without accumulation at the root of financialization. Which is to say, it is necessary to analyze financialization as the other side of a process of the value *production* affirmed starting from the crisis of the Fordist model, from the capitalist incapacity to suck surplus-value from immediate living labor, the wage labor of the factory. *The thesis that is being put forth here is that financialization is not an unproductive/parasitic deviation of growing quotas of surplus-value and collective saving, but rather the form of capital accumulation symmetrical with new processes of value production.* Today's financial crisis should then be interpreted as a *block* of capital accumulation rather than an implosive result of a process lacking capital accumulation.

Beyond the role of finance in the sphere of consumption, what has happened in these last 30 years is a veritable metamorphosis of production processes of this very surplus-value. There has been a transformation of valorization processes that witnesses the extraction of value no longer circumscribed to the place dedicated to the production of goods and services, but that extends beyond factory gates so to speak, in the sense that it enters directly into the sphere of the *circulation* of capital, that is, in the sphere of the exchange of goods and services. It is a question of extending the processes of value extraction to the sphere of reproduction and distribution—a phenomenon, let it be noted, well-known to women

for a long time. Evermore explicitly, in both economic theory and managerial strategies, the *externalization*
of production processes is spoken of, even "crowdsourcing" i.e., putting to use the crowd and its forms
of life (Jeff Howe, *Crowdsourcing. Why the power of the
crowd is driving the future of business*, New York, 2008).

Analyzing financial capitalism under this productive profile means talking about *bio-economy* or
biocapitalism, "whose form is characterized by its
growing connection to the lives of human beings.
Previously, capitalism resorted primarily to the functions of transformation of raw materials carried out by
machines and the bodies of the workers. Instead, biocapitalism produces value by extracting it not only
from the body functioning as the material instrument
of work, but also from the body understood as a
whole" (Vanni Codeluppi, *Il biocapitalismo. Verso lo
sfruttamento integrali di corpi, cervelli ed emozioni*,
Bollati Boringhieri, Torino, 2008). In our analysis of
the financial crisis, the reference to the whole of the
studies and theories of biocapitalism and cognitive
capitalism developed in these years is of a merely
methodological kind: here we are more interested in
highlighting the link between financialization and
the processes of value production that is at the basis
of the crisis-development of new capitalism than in
an accurate and exhaustive description of its salient
characteristics (moreover, already accomplished by a
growing number of scholars; a first effort in this sense

is the work by Andrea Fumagalli, *Bioeconomia e capitalismo cognitivo*, Carocci, Roma, 2007).

Empirical examples of the externalization of value production, of its extension into the sphere of circulation, are now abundant (of the most recent works on the consumer-as-producer phenomenon, see Marie-Anne Dujarier, *Le travail du consommateur. De McDo à eBay: comment nous coproduisons ce que nous achetons*, La découverte, Paris, 2008). Ever since the first phase of company outsourcing (subcontracts to suppliers and external consultants), which, beginning in the 1980s, saw the emergence of atypical labor and of second generation autonomous labor (freelance, entrepreneurs of themselves, former employees who became self-employed) along the lines of the "Toyota model," capitalist colonization of the circulation sphere has been nonstop, to the point of transforming the consumer into a veritable producer of economic value. *Coproduction,* where the individual is the coproducer of what he consumes, "is today at the heart of the strategies of public and private companies. They put the consumer to work in various phases of value creation. The consumer contributes to market creation, producing services, managing damages, and hazards, sorting litter, optimizing the fixed assets of suppliers and even administration. Coproduction concerns all mass services, specifically: retail, bank, transportation, free time, restaurant, media, education, health…" (Durajer, *op. cit.*, p. 8).

It may be useful, even at the risk of simplifying the analysis, to discuss the examples that have since become paradigmatic. Ikea, having delegated to the client a whole series of functions (individuation of the code of the desired item, locating the object, removal of shelves, loading it into the car, etc.), externalizes the labor of assembling the "Billy" bookshelf; this is externalizing consistent fixed and variable costs that are now held by the consumer with a minimal benefit in prices, but with large savings in terms of company costs. There are many other examples: software companies, beginning with Microsoft or Google, habitually beta test the new versions of their programs on consumers, but also the programs belonging to so-called open source software are improved by a multitude of people, by "productive consumers."

After the 2001 crisis, writes Tiziana Terranova, the new strategy of the new economy is "'social web' or 'web 2.0.' Web 2.0 businesses, O'Reilly says, all have something in common. Their success is based on their ability to attract masses of users who create a world of social relations on the basis of the platforms/environments made available by sites like Friendster, Facebook, Flickr, Myspace, SecondLife and Blogger. Nonetheless, O'Reilly underscores, the web 2.0 is not limited to these new platforms, but also involves applications like Google, in the extent to which they manage to harness and valorize user browsing; or other applications that again allow the extraction of surplus value from common actions like linking a site, flagging a blog post, modifying software, and so forth. [...] Web 2.0 is a winning model for investors, since it harnesses, incorporates, and valorizes the social and technological labor of users. The frontier of innovation of the capitalist valorization process in the new economy is the 'marginalization of waged labor and the valorization of free [user] labor,' which is to say an unpaid and undirected labor, but which is nonetheless controlled" (T. Terranova, *New economy, finanziarizzazione e produzione sociale del Web 2.0*, in A. Fumagalli, S. Mezzadra, *op. cit.* The cited work of Tim O'Reilly is *What Is Web 2.0. Design Patterns and Business Models for the Next Generation of Software*, 30/09/2005, http://www.oreillynet.com/pub/a/oreilly /tim/news/2005/09/30/what-is-web-20.html).

The first important consequence of the new processes of capital valorization is the following: the quantity of surplus-value created by new apparatuses of extraction is *enormous*. It is based on the compression of direct and indirect wages (retirement, social security cushions, earnings from individual and collective savings), on the reduction of socially necessary labor with flexible network company systems (precarization, intermittent employment), and on the creation of a vaster pool of free labor (the "free labor" in the sphere of consumption, circulation and reproduction, with a more intensified cognitive labor). The quantity of surplus-value, i.e., of unpaid labor, is at the root of the increase in the profits *not* reinvested in the production sphere, profits whose increase does not, as a consequence, generate the growth of stable employment, let alone wage increases.

Under this profile and in reference to the Marxist debate about the cause of the crisis (*La Brèche*), it is thus possible to partially agree with Alain Bihr's thesis according to which we have been in the presence of an "excess of surplus value" for quite some time but, unlike Bihr and Hudson (already cited), this is not the result of a lack of accumulation, of a lack of reinvestment of profits in constant and variable capital. The excess of surplus-value is, *instead*, the result of a *new accumulation process* that has been in place since the crisis of Fordism *in* the sphere of circulation and reproduction of capital. Francois Chesnais' objections to Alain Bihr's thesis stating that the excess of surplus-value did not just lead to a search for new market outlets—since a significant number of multinational American and European companies have in fact increased their direct investments abroad (in China, Brazil, and, with some difficulties, India)—would thus have to be amplified: direct investments, reflective of typical capital profit, have not been carried out only outside the economically developed countries, *but inside them*, namely, in the sphere of circulation and reproduction.

The relationship between accumulation, profits and financialization should be reinterpreted on the basis of the salient characteristics of post-Fordist production processes. The increase in profits fueling financialization was possible because, in biocapitalism, the very concept of accumulation of capital was transformed. It no longer consists, as in the Fordist period, of investment in constant and variable capital (wage), but rather of investment in *apparatuses* of producing and capturing value produced outside directly productive processes.

As Tiziana Terranova writes with regard to these new company strategies, "it is a question of attracting and individuating not just this 'free labor,' but also in some way various forms of possible surplus-value that can capitalize on the diffused desires of sociality, expression, and relation. In this model, the production of profit by companies would take place over and against the individuation and capture of a 'lateral' surplus-value (the sale of publicity, and the sale of data produced by the activity of users, the capacity to attract financial investments on the basis of visibility and the prestige of new global brands like Google and Facebook). In many cases, surplus-value resides in the saving of costs of this very labor, since the latter becomes 'externalized' to users (the externalization of analysis and beta testing of videogames or technical support to users)."

These crowdsourcing technologies, based on what Alexander Galloway called "protocological control," represent the new organic composition of capital, i.e., the relationship between constant capital (as the totality of "linguistic machines") dispersed in society and variable capital (as the totality of sociality, emotions, desires, relational capacity, and… "free labor") deterritorialized, despatialized, dispersed in the sphere of reproduction, consumption, forms of life and individual and collective imagination. New constant capital, differently from the system of (physical) machines typical of the Fordist age, is constituted, beyond information and communication technology (ICT), by a totality of immaterial organizational systems that suck surplus-value by pursuing citizen-laborers in every moment of their lives, with the result that the working day, the time of living labor, is excessively lengthened and intensified (Stephen Baker, "The Next. Companies May Soon Know Where Customers are Likely to be Every Minute of the Day," *Business Week*, March 9, 2009).

The "Google model," like the "Toyota model" 30 years ago, should be properly understood as a new *mode* of producing goods and services in the age of biocapitalism. It is a *model* of company organization that, having assumed the form of internet services in the sector, i.e., in the age of the new economy in the course of the second half of the 1990s, has been gradually asserted in all sectors of the economy, be they producers of immaterial services or material goods. In other words, it is not the nature of the product that determined the productive organization (or paradigm), but rather the relationship between the spheres of production and circulation, between production and consumption, that shapes the modalities of producing goods and services. The "Google model" is today proposed as a company strategy in order to save the American automobile industry, the industry that made the history of the twentieth century beginning with Henry Ford's revolution and that today is in the gravest of crises from every point of view (Laurent Carroué, "Le coeur de l'automobile américaine a cessé de battre," *Le monde diplomatique*, February, 2009).

Jeff Davis' book *What Would Google Do?*, of which *Business Week* published an excerpt (February 9, 2009), is significant in this regard because it shows how the possibility of overcoming this crisis depends on the capacity of the car industry to reestablish a direct, transparent, participatory, creative, emotive, and expressive relationship with automobile consumer-users. The creation of networks, or, as they are called in the internet world, communities of consumers, who coproduce innovation, diversification, and identification with the brand, on the basis of open source, shows how the "Google model" is being asserted outside the virtual universe, even in the hyper-material world of the automobile. It adds that this managerial revolution began 30 years ago, indeed beginning with the crisis of the Fordist model, a crisis overcome by applying productive strategies that are ever more present in the sphere of circulation and reproduction, i.e., in the sphere of *bios*, of life.

Moreover, the studies of *cognitive capitalism*, in addition to highlighting the centrality of cognitive/immaterial labor, of cooperation between brains beyond the separation of company and territory, between public and private spheres, between individuals and organization in the creation of added value, show the increasing loss of strategic importance of fixed capital (*physical* instrumental goods) and the transfer of a series of productive-instrumental functions to the living body of the workforce (Christian Marazzi, *Capitalismo digitale e modello antropogenetico del lavoro. L'ammortamento del corpo macchina*, in J. L. Laville, C. Marazzi, ed. M. La Rosa, F. Chicchi, *Reinventare il lavoro*, Sapere 2000, Rome, 2005).

"The economy of knowledge harbors a curious paradox. The prototype of each new good is costly for the companies because, in order to start producing and commercializing it, huge investments in research are necessary. But the next units cost little because it is simply a question of replicating the original and it is possible to do this inexpensively thanks to the advantages derived from delocalized production, from available technologies and digitalization processes. It follows that companies will concentrate their efforts and resources on the production of ideas, having to confront, however, the progressive tendency of the increase in costs" (Codeluppi, *op. cit.*, p. 24).

One of the main characteristics of cognitive capitalism is, in fact, the chasm between initially very high costs (particularly due to the investments in Research and Development, marketing, etc) necessary for continued invention/innovation of products and marginal costs of additional units of products introduced to the market, the costs tending toward zero. In fact, being able to be replicated at decreasing costs lies in fact in the very nature of products of high technological content and cognitive labor (on this subject, see the fundamental work by E. Rullani, *Economia della conoscenza. Creatività e valore nel capitalismo delle reti*, Carocci, Roma, 2004. Also important is the work *L'età del capitalismo cognitivo. Innovazione, proprietà e cooperazione delle moltitudini*, ed. by Yann Moulier Boutang, Ombre Corte, Verona, 2002).

This characteristic of cognitive capitalism refers to the theory of *growing earnings*, i.e., to the increase in profits originating in the drastic reduction of reproduction costs of goods. The theory of growing earnings, particularly relevant in an economy that has turned knowledge into a highly productive and competitive factor of production (*endogenous*, i.e., an integral part of the *normal* activity of companies), was masterly examined by David Warsh in his *Knowledge and the Wealth of Nations: a Story of Economic Discovery* (W. W. Norton, New York, 2006).

For the scope of our analysis, it will suffice to reiterate the example of the "pin factory" often used by the economists in order to explain the increase in the productivity of labor resulting from the division-specialization of labor. "Suppose," writes Warsh, "the pinmaker gets into the market early, expands, specializes in pinmaking by investing in new equipment and pinmaking R&D. He develops better steel, more attractive packaging, more efficient distribution channels. The bigger his market, the greater the specialization of this sort he can afford. He replaces workers with machines. The greater the specialization, the more efficient his production, the lower the price at which he can afford to sell his pins. The lower the price, the more pins he sells, and the more he sells, the higher his profits: a greater return for the same effort, hence increasing returns to scale" (p. 46).

Analyzed under this profile, Adam Smith's "pin factory" (that very much reminds us of today's multinational companies) evokes the tendency of the companies possessing the know-how accumulated in machines and living labor towards *monopoly*, that is, a situation where the first to arrive gets everything and the market is resupplied with pins "perhaps not in the quantity necessary to satisfy the demand." Something is in strident contradiction with the other (still major) interpretation of Adam Smith, according to which the "invisible hand," that is, the *free competition*, governing the market such that "no producer can prevail and if someone tries to increase prices, he is at once cut out, such that the price immediately returns to its 'natural value': there are as many pins on the market as needed by consumers." In other words, "the pin factory speaks of reduction of costs and increasing earnings. The invisible hand speaks, instead of increasing costs and decreasing earnings" (p. 70), and the two theorems, naturally, exclude each other.

However, increasing earnings are counterbalanced by the continued tendency of increasing production costs determined by a series of other factors, such as the growth of market exchange rates, the rapid technological obsolescence of productive facilities, increased consumer demand, the necessity of always producing new stimuli in order to incite the desire of wealthy consumers, the growth of the competition rate between companies, the competition between company messages and other messages circulating in society and the growing complexity of the social system (Codeluppi, *op. cit.*, pp. 25–26).

In order to confront the rise of costs, companies develop both forms of externalization of entire segments of activity to countries with low cost of labor, as well as processes of the creation of *scarcity* (by means of certificates, patents, copyrights) necessary to absorb the initial costs with monopolistic sales prices. Finally, they develop the reduction of direct investment in capital assets. For example, in order to reduce the initial costs, the companies "no longer think of purchasing capital equipment but rather borrow the physical capital they need in the form of a lease and charge it as a short-term expense, a cost of doing business" (Jeremy Rifkin, *The Age Of Access: The New Culture of Hypercapitalism, Where All of Life is a Paid-For Experience*, Putnam Publishing Group, 2000, p. 41).

The increase in the quantity of living labor not only reflects the transfer of the strategic means of production (consciousness, knowledges, cooperation) to the living body of labor-power, but allows one to explain the trend loss of the economic value of the classical means of production. It is thus not a mystery if the recourse to stock markets over the last few years was not aimed at investments immediately productive of an increase in the amount of employment and wage, but rather at the increase in shareholder value pure and simple. The auto-financing of investments in fixed capital assets and wages, should there be any, shows that the accumulation leverage has something to do with the monetization of value produced outside companies, i.e., inside society.

The increase in profits over the last 30 years is thus due to a production of surplus-value with accumulation, although an entirely new accumulation because it is external to classical productive processes. It is in this sense that the idea of a "becoming-rent of profit" (and, in part, wages themselves) is justified as a result of the capture of a value produced outside directly productive spaces. Today's system of production curiously resembles the eighteenth century economic circuit centered around farming and theorized by the physiocrats. In Quesnay's *Tableaux économique*, rent represents the quota of the net product, appropriated by the landlord, generated by agricultural labor of wage workers (including the labor of the capitalist tenant where income was considered in the same way as the wage of his workers and not, as it later will be defined by Smith and Ricardo, as profit). In the *Tableaux*, the physical instruments of production are not even taken into consideration. Quesnay defined the producers of instrumental goods (constant capital) as the active part of the *sterile* class, that is, as not producing any net product, to the extent that the production of instruments of labor does not add anything to the raw material used, but only *transforms* it.

The exclusion of constant capital, of instrumental goods, from the factors of production of net gain was certainly a mistake, as was later shown by the fathers of classical political economy on the wave of the first industrial revolution. The physiocrats' mistake was to consider agricultural labor the only productive labor because it produces things with things, and is thus quantitatively *measurable*. But, if it is true that the subsequent discovery of economic value of constant capital and its qualitative difference in respect to variable capital (that is, the discovery of *generic labor*, the labor *abstracted from* specific sectors where it is carried out) the physiocrats' mistake was a *productive* one, since it was at the basis of the epistemological leap that radically distinguished modernity from capitalism. That is, it was this error that would reveal the qualitative-subjective *separation* between capital and labor and the contradictory *relationship* between the two "factors of production" as the crisis-development leverage of nascent capitalism. From that moment on, capitalism has been *chasing* the subjective rearticulations of living labor, its struggles, its aspirations, and its new forms of cooperation.

It could be said that the forms of life undermining the social body are equivalent to land in Ricardo's theory of rent. Only that, unlike Ricardo's rent (absolute and differential), today's rent is subsumable to profit precisely *in virtue* of financialization processes themselves. Financialization, with its specific logic—particularly the autonomization of the production of money via money through directly productive processes—is the other face of the externalization of value production typical of biocapitalism. Financialization not only contributes to the production of the effective demand necessary for the *realization* of the product of surplus-value (i.e., it does not only create the mass of rent and consumption without which the growth of the GDP would be modest and stagnant) but also fundamentally *determines* continuous innovations and continuous productive leaps in biocapitalism, imposing on all companies—quoted or not—and on the whole of society its hyper-productive logics centered around the primacy of shareholder value. These productive leaps determined by financialization are systematically carried out through the "creative destruction" of capital, through successive extensions of valorization processes at the very heart of society with evermore sophisticated crowdsourcing models. Through closer and evermore frequent crises, access to social wealth, after having been structurally stimulated, is then destroyed again and again.

Starting with the crisis of Fordism in the 1970s, economic bubbles should thus be interpreted as moments of crisis within a long-term process of "capitalist colonization" of the sphere of circulation. This is a global process, that is it explains globalization as a process of subsuming growing quotas of global and local socio-economic peripheries in accordance with the logic of financial (bio)capitalism. The passage from imperialism to empire, i.e., from a relationship of dependence between development and underdevelopment where the economies of the South essentially functioned as *external* market outlets in addition to being the sources of downmarket raw material, to imperial globalization where the dichotomy between inside and outside breaks down, is also to be included in the capitalist logic of the externalization of value production processes. *Financialization represents the adequate and perverse modality of accumulation in this new capitalism.*

4

A CRISIS OF GLOBAL GOVERNANCE

Beginning in August 2007 with the explosion of sub-prime loans, the financial crisis looks more and more like a long-term crisis, a crisis paired with a credit crunch, banking bankruptcies, continuous interventions by monetary authorities not able to structurally influence the crisis; there are costly actions of economic revival, risks of insolvency of individual countries, deflationary pressures and possible violent returns of inflation, unemployment increases and income reduction. For all intents and purposes, this crisis is *historical*, in the sense that it contains all the contradictions accumulated over the course of the gradual financialization of economy that began with the crisis of Fordist accumulation (for an analysis of the deregulation of the banking system that began in the 1970s in the midst of the Fordist crisis, see Barry Eichengreen, "Anatomy of the Financial Crisis," *Vox*, http://www.voxeu.org/index.php?q=node/1684).

Nevertheless, the present crisis finds its moment of determination and acceleration in the Asian crisis of 1997–1999. Certainly, the Asian crisis was, in turn, preceded by a series of foreboding crises, such as the Mexican and Argentinian crises, the Russian and Brazilian crises, the crisis of Long Term Capital Management and the Japanese "lost decade," crises that Paul Krugman analyzed in 1998 in his *The Return of Depression Economics*, republished in 2008 with an update on the subprime loan crisis and the general banking crisis. However, the Asian crisis marked a change of regime in the international financial order from the moment the Southern and Asian countries decided—in order to overcome the crisis of excessive debt in dollars that caused real estate speculation and industrial overinvestment in local currency—to accumulate reserves of international currencies to protect themselves against the risk of subsequent destructive crises in the implicit stability of the global monetary financial system. This was a radical change in the economic model to the extent that, from growth stimulated by internal demand, Asian countries chose a model of growth based on exports. In this way, Asian countries went from being dollar debtors to creditors, particularly to the US. In order to accumulate foreign currencies, Asian countries adopted "predatory" policies in international commerce, resorting to strong devaluations, competitive deflation, and the limitation of internal consumption. If the opening of international commerce in countries like China and India is added to this scenario, it can be seen how the net result of an Asian turn is deflationary:

certainly deflationary for wages, which are suddenly effected by the redoubling of the global amount of active population, but also deflationary for industrial consumer goods produced and exported from China and, to a lesser yet qualitatively important extent, from India. Wage deflation "was, on the other hand, aggravated by the eruption of financial logic in the companies in the real sector of economy, through procedures like reacquisition of companies with debt and leverage effect (leveraged buy-outs, or LBO)" (Sapir, *op. cit.*, p. 5).

The risk of deflation became more and more real after the internet bubble crisis. In fact, starting in 2002, company debt redemption, having been massively accumulated in the expansive period of the internet bubble (1998–2000), compelled Alan Greenspan's Federal Reserve to pursue an expansive monetary policy. In order to avoid entering the vicious circle of deflation experienced by Japan in the 1990s, the American monetary authorities decided to keep interest rates low (around 1%) for a particularly long period, also because, with several important company bankruptcies since 2002 (Enron, to name just one), the expansive monetary policy could not reestablish the confidence of stock markets. In any case, *negative* real interest rates reinforce private indebtedness but, at the same time, caused banks to develop the panoply of financial instruments and the famous securitizations under accusation today (the now famous toxic assets) in order to increase credit volume.

The subprime real estate bubble begins in this context. Companies manage, at least partially, to redeem their debt thanks to negative real interest rates, while the domestic American economies become exponentially indebted (very often *urged* to do so). This increase in consumption through debt exasperates the American commercial deficit and, consequently, reinforces the monetary mercantilist policies of Asian countries even more. Asian countries would then sterilize their realized gains by buying massive amounts of dollars in order to avoid devaluation, which would damage their exports to the US, and then create Sovereign Funds with the gains in their budgets. These state funds, for a certain period, seemed to be able to resolve the crisis of Western banks. The deflationary tendency is also aggravated because the commercial gains of Asian countries (despite the sterilization measures taken) generate investments in these same exporting countries, investments that, in turn, improve the competitiveness of emerging countries not only through low labor costs but also through the quality of products and the higher added value.

The description, however schematic, of the dynamic that led to the subprime bubble burst shows that the crisis ripened within a precise global configuration of capitalist accumulation. Within this configuration and this international division of labor, financialization allowed *global* capital to grow thanks to the production of financial rents and consumer debts that endowed international exchanges with *systemic coherence*. Global economic growth, particularly after the internet bubble crisis and debt redemption on the part of companies after that, saw capital restructure itself with subsequent externalization processes. The aim here is to reduce the cost of living labor with increases in the quantity of surplus-value not correlated with increases proportional to investments in constant capital. In fact, particularly from 1998 to 2007, large companies (S&P 500) witnessed a continued and particularly high increase in non-reinvested profits (free cash flow margins), an accumulation of liquidity parallel to the high increase in consumption, both with reduced family savings and with recourse to indebtedness.

As always, the crises of capital break loose because of the same forces that determined their growth (the typical palindromic movement of the transaction cycle). But *this* crisis illuminates something unforeseen with regard to the preceding crises: the loss of capacity on the part of American monetary authorities, (even if they manage the international currency par excellence), to manage liquidities coming to their market as a result of the "mercantilist"-predatory monetary strategy used in Asian countries after the '97–'99 crisis. This specificity (in his day, Alan Greenspan spoke of "conundrum"), already pointed out by Michel Aglietta and Laurent Berrebi (*Désordres dans le capitalisme mondial*, Odile Jacob, Paris, 2007), refers to the consequences of a liquidity influx from developing countries and from the countries producing and exporting oil to the American bond market—particularly Treasury bonds and Fannie Mae and Freddie Mac bonds. The massive and continued liquidity influx from developing countries in fact *reduces* long-term interest rates on bonds, such as T-bills. In fact, when bonds (providing fixed income) increase in value because they are in high demand on the market, corresponding interest rates decrease proportionately in order to be able to ensure the same earning.

The reduction of long-term interest rates occurs *despite* the Fed's repeated attempts between 2004 and 2007 to stop the increase in the amount of credits with the increase in direct, short-term interest rates (that jump from 1% to 5.25%). "It is this very special situation of an inverted curve where long-term interest rates have become less than short-term rates—an atypical situation for such a long period—that made it so that the cost of credit remained very low for quite some time in the US, despite an evermore restrictive monetary policy" (Aglietta, *La crise*, p. 39). Able to borrow currency in bulk from money markets, banks have the means to give out loans with an ever higher risk to the domestic economies. Consequently, real estate prices in the US were rising until the fall of 2006 and until 2008 in various European countries (rising from 60% to 80% in France and redoubling over ten years in England and Spain).

The crisis of governance of the American monetary authorities is thus explained as the incapacity to manage the effects of liquidity influx from the rest of the world, especially from developing countries. In fact, the post-crisis Asian globalization obscures the increase in risk of crisis internal to the transaction cycle within developed countries because the reduction of premiums on bond risks (long-term bonds) increasingly exposes the financial sector to the valorization of all patrimonial assets. Once again, in this process, it is the *temporal dimension* that is central in the analysis of the crisis. The signs of a real estate crisis were already manifesting themselves in 2004, so much that the Fed began its race to increase interest rates. But the influx of foreign liquidity annulled this monetary policy so that the bubble was swelling undeterred until August 2007. And not just that: already in the middle of 2006, real estate prices halted their rise to then drop towards the end of the same year. But the bubble popped in August 2007 when the rating agencies finally decided to declassify (now toxic) assets issued in credit; which is to say, a year after the inversion of the transaction cycle (to confirm this reconstruction of the post-Asian crisis, see "When a Flow Becomes a Flood," *The Economist,* January 24, 2009).

In other words, the crisis of monetary governance reveals a *gap* between the economic and financial-monetary cycles, in the sense that the former develops in a shorter time than the latter. In the cycle of the real economy, like in all business cycles, the crisis begins at the moment when the inflationary increase in prices (for example, of real estate) provokes a *falling* increase of demand. Demand grows, but grows ever more slowly because actualizing the flow of future incomes no longer justifies the "irrational" increase in prices on goods on which the bubble is concentrated.

In "old" economic cycles, this slowdown was usually manifested by near-full employment. For the banking system, this means a slowdown in the rhythm of repaying the credits lavished in the phase preceding the cycle, the phase during which credit is easy and super-speculation is unleashed on the wave of the increase in profits (the so-called financial overtrading). In approaching full employment, companies and indebted consumers start, however, to show signs of difficulty repaying their debts because the amount of sales (for the companies struggling with the drop in demand) and available incomes (for domestic economies confronted by inflation) begins to fall. For banks, both secondary and central ones, this is the moment to increase the interest rates.

The overtrading and super-speculation preceding the inversion of the transaction cycle are nothing other than the creation of earnings *extrinsic* to the production of goods and services, of a demand *additional* to the one created directly inside the economic circuit. Overtrading favors the spending of a virtual income still waiting to be realized. Under this profile, the multiplication of securitized assets has certainly been at the basis of overtrading, to the extent that it allowed for the creation of virtual incomes on the basis of the presupposition, later revealed as entirely unrealistic, of their future realization. But when overtrading topples over into its opposite, that is, when it goes from the phase of easy money characterized by a credit crunch, this additional demand collapses, it vaporizes very quickly, and the economic system enters into recession. Companies in every sector are no longer able to sell, warehouses accumulate more and more supplies, and domestic economies begin to experience the reduction of their income due to lay-offs and/or the difficulty maintaining consumption at the same levels as those of the preceding phase of the cycle. This is the moment when the crisis is revealed as the crisis of *overproduction* on a wide scale. This is also the moment when, in order to reestablish an operative balance between demand and supply, one very often turns to *scrapping* of unsold surplus or, in any case, to its devalorization. The violence of crises consists in this *destruction of capital*, a destruction that in biocapitalism strikes the totality of human beings, their emotions, feelings, affects, which is to say the "resources" put to work by capital (for a description of the role of finance in the expansion-recession dynamic of the economic cycle based on Hyman Minsky's theory, see Robert Barbera, *The Cost of Capitalism: Understanding Market Mayhem and Stabilizing Our Economic Future*, McGraw-Hill, 2009).

The collapse of overtrading manifests itself in its entire *social* dimension, i.e., as a phenomenon of *realization*, of selling the quantity of goods and services (and the quantity of value embodied in them) that concerns not just one sector or another (if this were the case, we would see an inter-sectorial compensation), but *all* the sectors at once. But the fact that the overturning of super-speculation—that is, the crunch to the point of zeroing the additional demand created by the mechanism of overtrading—is at the root of overproduction also shows that the imbalance between demand and supply is a *structural* characteristic of the economic cycle. In other words, the supply of goods and services is *at the root* of excessive demand. Say's law, postulating a fundamental identity between supply and demand, is thus false, not just because the explosion of the crisis involves rushing to banking windows and the deferral of spending on the part of the domestic economies (so-called retention), but also because demand and supply are structurally imbalanced. If this weren't the case, the collapse of overtrading would reestablish the equality between demand and supply—something that never happens. The crisis reveals the excess of supply over demand, latent overproduction inside the transaction cycle. It is for this reason that the crisis calls into being anti-cyclical actions tending to create new additional demand, measures that only the state can implement, since there is a general flight in the private economy. No mechanism of market autoregulation can alone reestablish the conditions for overcoming the crisis.

Financial globalization, as we've seen, *defers* the rendering of accounts, that is, the inversion of the cycle, precisely because the amount of credit to companies and consumers can keep increasing despite the signs of the inversion of the cycle of the real economy (for instance, the prices on real estate beginning to drop). All of this despite the trend in the balance of payments that contributes to hiding the symptoms of the imminent crisis. In fact, until the massive influx of savings from developing countries, in search of not high, but secure earnings, is counterbalanced by the flow of American investments directed abroad (which have earnings greater than the internal ones and which increase the profits of US companies, especially when the dollar is low relative to other currencies), the American monetary authorities can avoid facing the *all the while evident* problem of international commercial imbalances.

Moreover, the temporal gap, where the crisis of American monetary governance is reversed, is at the root of the transformation of regional crises into *immediately* global ones. Certainly, this is due to the dissemination of risks and toxic assets that infects bank portfolios, insurances, hedge and equity funds, retirement funds, and everyone's investments in this period. But, at a closer look, it is a question of a crisis that goes well beyond the world diffusion of toxic assets. As shown by the total inefficiency of all the measures undertaken up to now by governments all over the world in order to recapitalize the banking and insurance system with huge injections of liquidity.

It is thus possible to claim that the crisis of monetary governance explains *only* one part, only the *beginning* of the crisis we are living in. Proof is that, at the worst moment of the financial crisis—October 2008—contrary to what everyone expected, the dollar *appreciated* against all other currencies. "The anomaly is that the dollar has grown stronger over the course of these last weeks against almost all other currencies" (Eichengreen, *op. cit.*). However, it is possible that, like after the reevaluation of the dollar in August 2007 (in the midst of the subprime crisis!), the dollar starts to devalue again, with inevitable inflationary effects on a global scale (caused, like over the course of 2007–2008, by strong increases in oil and food prices). This makes us suppose that the global imbalances between structurally deficient countries (the US and England), and countries in surplus, such as developing countries (but also Germany and Japan), are destined to last a long time still. A long time, i.e., *beyond* the emergency measures and the redefinition of the banking and financial rules that—from the internet crisis until the subprime bubble burst—allowed the flow of liquidity towards the US to produce the leverage effect of credit that we've seen. As a high official of the China Bank Regulatory Commission, Luo Ping, told a journalist of the *Financial Times*, "we hate you guys, but there is nothing much we can do" except continue to buy American public debt (cited in Bill Powell, "China's Hard Landing," *Fortune*, March 16, 2009).

It would suffice to pose a seemingly provocative question: what else could the American monetary authorities and the rest of the world do? Certainly, with hindsight, it is possible to say anything; it is possible, for instance, to invoke (precisely *ex post*) prudential monetary policies, increases in banking reserves, better quality control of issued assets, stricter rules on securitizations based on subprime mortgage loans, and so on. But what could have the American monetary authorities and the central banks of developing countries have done, the former being confronted with the risk of deflation, the latter recovering, shattered, from the '97–'99 crisis? The answer is: nothing other than what has been done. Suffice to say that if the Fed had effected a more restrictive monetary policy in order to restrain or lessen the foreign deficit of the current balance, the result would have been a recession in the US and, consequently, in developing countries as well. On top of that, how could the Fed have justified a restrictive monetary policy when the problem was not inflation, but rather deflation?

Let us only recall that a peculiar characteristic of today's financial capitalism and the monetary policy proper to it is the impossibility of externally managing what occurs inside the economico-financial cycle. The theoretical analyses of André Orléan, Michel Aglietta, Robert Shiller, Hyman Minsky, George Soros and Fédéric Lordon, to cite the best, show how, in order to interpret the behavior of financial operators on the basis of the value-at-risk models, it is impossible to distinguish between cognitive and manipulative functions, between economic rationality and mimetic behavior of the multiplicity of actors. The neoclassical theory of rational expectations based on perfect information and market transparency has, for a long time, been beside the point, because it removes a central factor of the financial markets, i.e., the intrinsic *uncertainty* that characterizes them, an uncertainty evermore based on the diminishing dichotomy between real and financial economies. In other words, the hypothesis of "efficient markets" has to be substituted by that of "market instability," a structural instability within the public nature of currency, as "public good," breeds collective behaviors (such as panic) that have little to do with the rationality of individual economic operators, but that are, however, an integral part of market functioning.

According to George A. Akerlof and Robert Shiller, the rationality of *Homo economicus* explains only a quarter of relevant economic actions. The rest is guided by the animal spirits already described by Keynes, i.e., it is the aptitude of individuals to "flirt with ambiguity" which guides decisions about investments when uncertainty prevents one from being rational (*Animal Spirits: How Human Psychology Drives the Economy, and Why it Matters for Global Capitalism*, Princeton University Press, Princeton, 2009). "These non-economic motivations are mood-related and subject to spontaneous changes that drag economy up and down. If rationality is a good guide in normal times, it is less so in situations of positive (economic bubbles) and negative (crises) stress. We neither anticipated the crisis nor are we able to overcome it because we do not take this factor into account" (Giorgio Barba Navaretti, *Travolti dagli Animal Spirits*, "Il Sole 24 Ore," March 8, 2009). The fact is that the times have not been normal for a while now and this shows that from 1985 until today, i.e., from the liberal turn imparted to economies by market deregulation, there has been a financial and/or monetary crisis, on average, every two and half years. This is enough to definitively put in crisis the fundamental presuppositions of the neo-classical theory, according to which "markets realize the best allocation of capital and the best management of risk."

In fact, there is a particular ontological weakness in the models of probability calculation used to evaluate risks due to the *endogenous* nature of the interactions between the financial operators (see André Orléan, *La notion de valeur fondamentale est-elle indispensable à la théorie financière?, Regards croisés sur l'économie. Comprendre la finance contemporaine*, March 3, 2008). This explains the "evaluation errors" of risk not so much, or not only, as mistakes attributable to the conflict of interests scandalously typical of rating agencies, but as the expression of an (ontological) impossibility of making rules or meta-rules able to discipline markets in accordance with so-called rational principles. All the more so when, according to the methods used to establish the value of financial assets, like the ones based on the new accounting norms (International Financial Reporting Standards, IFRS, secured by Basel II), the fair value of assets is calculated on the basis of the conflict between their market value and the value at which the asset is being negotiated, that is, its historical value (the method used to establish this valuation is called "mark to market"). The problem posed by these methods of valuation is that, since fair values act as a reference to calculate the value of a patrimonial asset—in the same way as a private citizen who calculates his *real* assets, including the *current* market value of his real estate—there is a strong urge to increase asset value by increasing debt: "in an accounting of this kind, the debt of assets buyers seems weak because it is guaranteed, collaterally, by assets whose value grows faster than debt. Thus, bankers do not understand the risk because they see market values as indicators. But this risk, nonetheless very real, does not at all appear in the variables that are measured on the basis of accounting rules considered a good standard" (Aglietta, *op. cit.*, pp. 18–19). It is a question of a veritable urge to indebtedness, precisely as it occurs over the course of the period of the greatest financialization of the economy. *And this according to the very rules established on an international level by those that are supposed to regulate the markets!*

It is possible to maintain that the crisis of governance has its origin in a double resistance: on one hand, the resistance of developing countries to every attempt to keep them in a subordinate position in respect to developed countries, a resistance that led them to modify their growth model after the Asian crisis. The Asian export-oriented model has in fact transformed the amount of savings not reinvested internally into *financial rent*—the rent realized by redirecting liquidity towards the outside; on the other hand, there has been the resistance of the

American domestic economies that have played the card of *social rent*, a kind of "with and against" the financialization of the economy. For a certain period of time, American families were acting, as financially unstable as it may have been, on the terrain of social property rights, the right to a house and the (indebted) consumption of goods and services. And this was, we would do well to recall, in a period of state disinvestment in the fundamental sectors such as education and professional training, disinvestment that caused the impressive increase in the cost of education, forcing families to go in debt in order to allow their own children to study. Private spending deficit, far from being the reflection of an all-American tendency to live beyond one's own means, is a phenomenon that has its roots in the liberal turn in the beginning of the 1980s and in the crisis of the Welfare State that followed it (on this subject, see Colin Crouch, "What Will Follow the Demise of Privatised Keynesianism," *The Political Quarterly*, No. 4, October–December 2008).

5

GEOMONETARY SCENARIOS

Crisis is the capitalist way for restoring economic order to the social and potentially political dimension of the resistance matured during the accumulation phase of the cycle. However, this crisis exploded on the basis of such a tangle of contradictions and rigidity on a global scale that Keynesian intervention on a regional scale is hardly able to undo them. It is thus obvious that overcoming the crisis is possible only if the actions of economic revival are inscribed in precise geopolitical and geomonetary strategies.

There are, essentially, three medium-term (from 5 to 10 years) scenarios which are extrapolated from the current crisis: "The first is founded on the US-China coupling (Chimerica), thus in a pact between the dollar and the yuan. The second extends the game to Russia and Western European powers, especially Germany and France, bound by a special agreement between Euroland and ruble (Eurussia). Thus determining, parallel to the Chino-American axis, the premises of a super Bretton Woods, a full agreement between all the major powers. The third scenario is the exacerbation of imbalances (beginning with the old Europe mayonnaise going bad and ongoing conflicts) to the point of rendering the system completely ungovernable. The catastrophes pile up to then reproduce August 1914, this time on a nuclear and planetary scale" (Lucio Caracciolo "L'impera senza credito," *Limes*, 5, 2008).

All these scenarios are based upon the inevitability of the decline of American hegemony, the decline of the *empire without credit*, the formula describing the paradox of the largest world power that is also the largest global debtor. The "self-evident" hypothesis of the American decline can be legitimately doubted if it is true that the crisis strikes the Asian countries in a particularly grave way, from China to Singapore, from Japan to South Korea ("Asia's Suffering," *The Economist*, January 31, 2009), while the US continues to be, as paradoxical as it may seem, one of the most secure places to invest one's savings.

Today's crisis ripened within a complex geo-monetary order that witnessed the multiplicity of actors bound to one another by autoreferential interests. China can maintain that the Americans should save more, but only as long as greater savings do not not affect its exports to the US. And the Americans can ask the Chinese how they managed, repeatedly in the past and, evermore timidly, even now, to reevaluate their currency and increase their internal consumption, but Americans are wary of restraining the purchase of T-bills by the Chinese. On the other hand, this crisis is already provoking a strong reduction in the net flow of private capital to the emerging countries (in 2009, it will not exceed $165 billion, less than half of the $466 billion of 2008 and a fifth of the capital flow of 2007). For their part, the actions of tax stimulus and rescuing the bankrupt Western banks can only produce the crowding out of the emerging markets and those of Eastern Europe. These actions would thus increase, on top of all of that, their Public debt service. This, let it be noted, can cause some Asian countries to try to protect themselves by increasing their currency reserves even more and investing their savings in the debt of the more developed economies, reiterating in such a way the same dynamics that favored the US credit explosion. In other words, the fundamental imbalances at the root of the crisis-development of financial capitalism of recent years are destined to persist for quite a lot of time, as Martin Wolf maintains on the pages of *Financial Times* ("Why G20 leaders will fail to deal with the big challenge," *FT*, April 1, 2009).

Thus, it is not the decline of the American empire that compels one to try the way of international cooperation in order to better manage global imbalances, but rather the fact that this crisis is destined to last a long time without any country being able to assume the role of leader in the world economy. As David Brooks said in an article that appeared in the *International Herald Tribune*, August 2, 2008, in today's global system, that which paralyzes capitalism is the impossibility of decision. The dispersion of power "should, in theory, be a good thing, but in practice, multipolarity means that more groups have effective veto power over collective action. In practice, this new pluralistic world has given rise to globosclerosis, an inability to solve problem after problem." In other words, the crisis radically undermined the very concept of unilateral and multi-lateral economico-political hegemony, i.e., that which compels one to explore new forms of multilateral world governance.

The first step in this direction is to ensure the emerging countries, and not just the Asian ones, that in case of a liquidity crisis they will not be left alone. The Fed's offer, in October, of a line of credit to four developing countries, even though these same countries already had abundant reserves, should be interpreted as an innovation in this direction. The objective is to better coordinate the actions of political economy to reorient the flows of capital so as to stimulate internal demand in developing countries, without, however, jeopardizing the monetary balance between the dollar and other currencies. It is worth noting that this strategy includes countries in the European zone, since Germany is also structurally in commercial excess and thus has all the interest to pursue policies of a revival of internal demand in order to counteract the drop of the external demand.

We should also note that the implementation of this geopolitical-monetary strategy is seeing, for the time being, the IMF play an entirely marginal role. The amounts in play well exceed the financial availability of the Fund. As a matter of fact, in the medium-long term, such an operative reinvention of the IMF (most importantly, a consistent increase in its liquidity, the increase of $500 billion decided on by the G20 and an internal redistribution of power from the US to the emerging countries) will reveal itself as necessary for the simple reason that the US cannot guarantee in the medium term to help developing countries with "precautionary" lines of credit. The construction of a super Bretton Woods with the IMF as its new armed hand, repeatedly invoked by the French President Sarkozy, must reckon with a characteristic of the Fund that sums up the gist of neoliberal American politics in the last decades.

It concerns an article, highly valued in the US, in the statues of the Fund, the obligation to the convertibility into a capital account (a convertibility that Keynes, during the preparatory work on the Bretton Woods agreements, resisted with all his force) where before there was only the convertibility into a current account. "And yet, the difference between the two notions is essential. In the second, the accent is on the flows of currencies that cover real transactions, on exchanges of goods and services, on tourist flows or the ones that still correspond to the repatriation of the incomes of the immigrants. In the first notion, all the portfolio operations, all the possible instruments of speculation, are authorized" (Sapir, *op. cit.*, p. 3).

The idea of a super Bretton Woods would be to cancel the obligation to convert into a capital account. This convertibility has, since the 1980s, represented the precondition of international market liberalization and the accumulation of global imbalances that repeatedly produced the financial crises of the last 30 years. Today even the IMF recognizes that this freedom of movement of capital significantly contributed to the destabilization of the system of commercial exchanges and international financial flows. However, the removal of the convertibility obligation into a capital account from the statutes of a hypothetical new IMF—that has as its fundamental objective the reestablishment of the *economic sovereignty* of nations and the symmetry of exchange relations guaranteed by a supranational monetary system—would have the inevitable consequence of disabling the apparatus that ensured, although with an impressive accumulation of contradictions and financial drifts, the development and affirmation of biocapitalism.

First off, the US would no longer be able to profit from the massive liquidity influx from the emerging countries which, as we've seen, allowed American capital to make consumption explode through the debt of American families. However one evaluates the hypothesis of a new Bretton Woods, it is certain that a reform of it in this sense would have spectacular effects on a model of society that, having dismantled the Welfare State, turned consumption and private indebtedness into the motor of its *modus operandi*. "The breaking point between the partisans of the old disorder and the partisans of a real reconstruction of the financial monetary system will be concentrated on two questions: the control of capital and of the forms of protectionism that allow one to avoid importing the depressive effects of the policies of a few countries" (Sapir, *op. cit.*, p. 32).

For the moment, the willingness of the Chinese government to continue purchasing assets of the American State does not seem to be in question (over the last years, China purchased 2 trillion dollars in American T-bills), but the same Chinese government voiced the hypothesis of a radical reform of the international monetary system in order to escape from the "dollar trap," that is, from the real risk of one of its devaluations (on this subject, see Zhou Xiuaochuan, governor of the central Chinese bank, *Reform the International Monetary System*, http://www.pbc.gov.cn/english). "The Chinese willingness," wrote Alfonso Tuor, "has, however, a price and this price is very high, especially for the US. Beijing asks for the reform of the international monetary system (a new Bretton Woods) with the objective of creating supranational exchange currency in place of the dollar. The Chinese authorities think that this function could be accomplished by the Special Drawing Rights of the IMF" ("Chi pagherà il conto della crisi?," *Corriere del Ticino*, March 27, 2009). Despite the hypothesis of reform, the mere call to do so has immediately destabilized the dollar on the currency markets, making it clear that this would entail the loss of the hegemony of the American currency in favor of the institution of a supranational currency (Special Drawing Rights), a synthetic monetary unity constituted by a totality of national currencies.

However, let it be recalled that the Special Drawing Rights are not a real supranational currency, but rather a unity of account comprised of other national currencies (dollar, euro, yen and sterling). This means that the idea of escaping from the trap of the dollar in which China finds itself after years of investing its own currency reserves in American T-bills can only be understood as desire on the part of the Chinese monetary authorities to *diversify* their own currency reserves, in other words, to reduce the detention of the dollar in favor of other national currencies, such as the euro, the yen, or the sterling. The reduction of the dollar detention would entail the devaluation of the American currency, a devaluation that would certainly damage Chinese exports.

The fact that, at least at the moment, neither the Chinese nor the Americans discuss the fundamental imbalance between the countries in export surplus and the developed countries in deficit (US and UK) renders a reform of the international monetary system highly problematic on this basis.

As Joseph Halevi wrote, commenting on the results of the G20 summit in London on April 2, "In the *Financial Times* of March 31st, Martin Wolf set down a straightforward criterion to evaluate the outcomes of the G20 meeting in London. Will they decide, he asked, to put forward a plan to shift world demand from the countries with a balance of payments deficit to those with a surplus? Wolf's hunch was that they would not even attempt to approach the issue. His guess turned out to be correct. As noted by the *New York Times*, the G20 has agreed to endow the IMF with 1.1 trillion dollars in the event of developing countries falling into balance of payments crises and needing loans. Yet, the paper points out, the G20 has made no provision to stimulate world demand. [...] The G20 didn't even address, let alone untie, the knot highlighted by Martin Wolf in the *Financial Times*. To really untie the knot, however, it is absolutely necessary to put an end to wage deflation in the Eurozone and to radically reorient the productive structures of the Japanese and Chinese economies" ("G20 and Inter-capitalist Conflicts," first published in *Il manifesto*, April 4, 2009).

This crisis marks, in fact, the end of the possibility of continually compensating the internal savings of the countries in surplus with the internal indebtedness of the countries in deficit. "Two years ago," wrote Paul Krugman, "we lived in a world in which China could save much more than it invested and dispose of the excess savings in America. That world is gone" ("China's Dollar Trap," *New York Times*, April 3, 2009). If one indeed wanted to reform the international monetary system in order to avoid reproducing fundamental imbalances on a global scale, it would be necessary to go in the direction of the institution of a real supranational currency, a pure vehicle of national purchase powers, like the Bancor unsuccessfully proposed by Keynes at Bretton Woods in 1944 or like the supranational currency for years theorized by the French economist Bernard Schmitt.

In this perspective, what is at stake are the possibilities or impossibilities of overcoming the ongoing crisis *politically*, rather than economically. The block of capitalist accumulation on a global scale should be interpreted in the light of these contradictory forces, with, on the one hand, the possibility that this crisis will last a very long time or at least will be systematically followed by similar crises, and, on the other hand, the possibility that, in order to overcome the crisis, the international monetary system is redefined in the name of national sovereignty and/or regional poles and the symmetry of commercial exchanges

(Martin Wolf, "Why President Obama Must Mend a Sick World Economy," *Financial Times*, January 21, 2009).

In the meantime, we would do well to watch how much of the New Deal the Obama administration will be able to accomplish. Investments in health with the reform of health insurance and investments in education, represent by far the two actions that generate major growth of employment, much more than tax cuts. Yet, today there are no transmission channels of the most available income to the demand of consumer goods (Michael Mandel, "The Two Best Cures For the Economy," *Business Week*, March 23–30, 2009). Among the different actions of the economic revival plan (*Financial Stability Plan* or FSP), there is one in particular that immediately merits close observation: the *Homeowner Affordability & Stability Plan*. On one hand, this measure wants to revive housing demand by lowering mortgage rates and making conventional loans more accessible by injections of liquidity to Fannie Mae and Freddie Mac. On the other hand, it authorizes bankruptcy judges to modify the loans taken by owners of insolvent houses. This action constitutes a precedent of historical import, since, in the US, loans for primary residences are currently the only ones that cannot be modified in bankruptcy courts (James C. Cooper, "Job One: Build a Floor Under Housing," *Business Week*, March 9, 2009).

As a whole, it is an innovative financial action with regard to all the other measures taken to rescue the banking and insurance system in the FSP—interventions that so far have proved to be decisively ineffective, or veritable fiascos, in Paul Krugman's words. The provision of mortgage refinance funds for American families is, in fact, the only technical action that will restore value to the derivative assets that are clogging up the world banking system today. Such an intervention would be without immediate effects on the public deficit, as the financing is spread over 30 years of loan contracts. In other words, the plan anticipates saving about 4 million families from foreclosure on their houses, but in such a way that a concrete value of the derivative securitized assets is re-established. The same plan allows the saving of many more banks than the emergency measures undertaken so far. The principle is clear: *begin from the base in order to reform the monetary system.*

In fact, beyond the technical aspect and the all-American specificity of the intervention to help homeowners who had fallen into the trap of easy loans, what counts in this measure is the principle, the *philosophy* that is at its basis. It lends itself to many considerations. In the first place, this action raises, at least incipiently, the question of the *right to social ownership* of a common good, a right that in all evidence is imposing itself on the right to private ownership as the only right conceivable today. In other words, if up until today, the access to a common good had taken the form of *private debt*, from now on it is legitimate to conceive (and reclaim it) the same right in the form of *social rent*. In financial capitalism, social rent assumes the form of redistribution, the way in which society gives everyone the right to live with dignity. As such, social rent is articulable on many terrains, particularly on that of education and access to knowledge in the form of the right to a *guaranteed education income*.

In the second place, this New Deal action of the new American democratic administration seems to be able to conjoin two levels, two plans that usually conflict with each other. On one hand, there is *local* intervention, with help oriented to a determined level of demand aggregated by intervening precisely where the crisis destroys incomes, job positions, and existences. On the other hand, this action has a *global* dimension to the extent that it aims at restoring economic value to financial instruments that, by definition, are created to be immersed in the global financial circulation, i.e., in portfolios of institutions and investment funds of every kind. One of the worst risks of this crisis is, in fact, the inward closure of nation-states, the race to competitive devaluations in order to regain bits of market by taking them away from others with protectionist actions. This is usually how wars break out.

Finally, this action has the absolutely crucial dimension of *time*, the fact being that the help to families in the form of the guarantee to a social rent is a veritable investment in the future. As we said, the interventions from the base not only allow one to avoid instantaneous and massive increases in the public debt, but these interventions are carried out on a *long* temporal horizon, a horizon within which the qualitative development of the new generation can be better ensured with investments in early childhood, in school and in entering the job market.

Taking time means giving each other the means of inventing one's own future, freeing it from the anxiety of immediate profit. It means caring for oneself and the environment in which one lives, it means growing up in a socially responsible way. To overcome this crisis without questioning the meaning of consumption, production, and investment is to reproduce the preconditions of financial capitalism, the violence of its ups and downs, the philosophy according to which "time is everything, man is nothing." For man to be everything, we need to reclaim the time of his existence.

AFTERWORD

From the bankruptcy of Lehman Brothers in the fall of 2008 to the G20 Summit in Toronto in June 2010, the crisis of financial capitalism has deepened and become even more complicated. In two years we've gone from state bailouts of banks, insurance companies, financial institutions and entire industrial sectors to the so-called "crisis of sovereign debt." The latter is the result of states taking responsibility for salvaging banks, the massive defiscalization of capital and of the high incomes of the last 15 years, the reduction of fiscal revenue typical of recessions, and the increase in costs tied to social welfare and in the interest on debt paid to Treasury bond holders.

In the same period, we've seen a process of economic and political concentration and reinforcement of the banks bailed out by the state who have exploited low interest rates to increase profits by directly and almost exclusively investing in the stock market and in state bonds. This has allowed banks to pay back the aid received in the heat of the crisis, thus freeing them from any political interference and putting them back into a position of dictating the conditions for recovery. Three years from the subprime bust, the political power of banking institutions has grown to such a point as to mitigate and slowdown the application of the most urgent legislative reforms in the sector, in particular the separation of commercial and investment banks (following in the footsteps of the Glass-Steagall Act of 1933) found in the "Dodd-Frank US Financial Regulation" voted on in June 2010, with the result that the financial-banking system will continue to be "too interconnected to let it fail" for a long time to come.

The banks, both public and private, highly exposed to debt—and still holding toxic bonds inherited from the speculative wave of subprime mortgages—in countries like Greece, Portugal, Spain, Ireland and Italy, are at the origin of the financial aid of the EU and the IMF to neighboring countries and the severe austerity measures imposed on their governments. The aid provided to indebted states are actually measures to bail out major European banks, in particular German and French ones. It is "recapitalization" masked in a phase in which, just like during the American subprime crisis, banks no longer trust one another because of the opaqueness of their accounts, the interbank market is practically blocked and the threat of selling off public bonds—hounded by the devaluation of the Euro—is provoking the fall of those same bonds, increasing interest rates. These in turn further burden the cost of debt and the deficit of the most indebted countries. The result of the stress tests made public on 23 July 2010, according to which only 7 European banks out of the 91 banks tested wouldn't be able to face a hypothetical financial shock, didn't substantially change the big picture, leaving banks exposed to the stress tests of the market for now. The net result of this "financial Keynesism" in which central banks monetize the growing demand of the financial-banking sector at the expense of investments aid at growth and employment, is the continuing crisis.

In the US, ever since the Federal Reserve concluded its program of acquiring bonds tied to real estate credit in March 2010, we've witnessed the shutting down of the securities market, thus limiting banks' possibility to package the credit paid in bonds to sell on the market. This, in turn, pushes American banks to restrict the criteria for credit concession even more. In Europe, the fact that the Central Bank has become the main source of financing for the banking system, is forcing banks to restrict their credit policies. It follows that, even if interest rates defined by central banks are close to zero and monetary policy is expansive, credit in the economy is still rationed. We are prisoners of a "liquidity trap" where the low cost of money doesn't kick start consumption and investments, all the more so when everyone keeps waiting for an improbable return of inflation and the relative increases in interest rates—a situation that Japan already experienced in the 1990s. Together, tight credit and austerity measures are determining a deflationary spiral that, as Paul Krugman maintains, can lead to a depression similar to those following the Panic of 1873 and the crisis in 1929–1931.

This picture is even more complicated when we look at it geopolitically. The clash between the US, Europe and developing countries, was evident at the Toronto G20 Summit. The Obama administration asked countries with strong commercial progress (Germany, China and Japan) to adopt expansive measures to sustain economic revival and substitute for American efforts, but Europe decided to maintain restrictive fiscal policies in order to face the crisis of trust over the sustainability of the public debt of its member states. The conclusion was a *de facto* null.

The US has exhausted the margins of "Keynesian" financial maneuvering. Its deficit is getting higher and higher and the Fed finds itself obliged to keep printing money in order to avoid a second recession. This is triggering a dangerous carry trade, with investors who go into dollar debt at a low cost and invest in bonds with higher returns. The only support to American and European recovery from the 2008–2009 recession consisted in America's expansive monetary and fiscal policies, but even these have proven to be ineffective on a short to midterm basis, as the persistence of high unemployment and the reemergence of the real estate market crisis after state aid stopped both demonstrate.

In Europe, the depreciation of the euro isn't able to counterbalance the depressive effects of the austerity measures taken by most EU countries, favoring only economically strong countries like Germany, whose exportations are mostly directed outside the eurozone. The policies of European governments converge on the adoption of "competitive disinflation" with draconian reductions in public employment, social welfare costs and salaries, but diverge from a strategic point of view. The political divergences between Germany and France are real and concern the definition of the size of the European block, fiscal harmonization policies, the relationship with the Central European Bank and the measures adopted towards countries that don't respect budget discipline. It is a power struggle between a France that has lost its position on the international market and a Germany that wants to dominate Europe with austere economic policy.

The crisis of sovereign debt has revealed what the creation of the eurozone was able to hide over the last few years: the fracture between industrially strong countries like Germany and its hinterland, geared towards exportation, and neighboring countries of the eurozone, Romania, Poland, the Baltic states and Hungary, whose economic growth depends on the reinvestment of commercial surplus in both public and private sectors by central countries.

This European circuit is similar to the one established between the US and China over these last few years, in which countries with commercial surplus invest their savings in T-bills issued to cover the debt of deficit countries rather than investing them domestically in wage increases and social welfare. As noted, the American subprime crisis matured inside this particular economic and financial cycle, thanks to the securitization of real estate mortgages, the latter facilitated by low interest rates on American T-bills resulting from the influx of Chinese capital. The European circuit has worked more or less in the same way, except that in Europe there is only one currency while in the US-China circuit there are two. This is no small difference because the internal structural imbalances of the eurozone don't leave room to form differentiated governance, like the choice to stimulate internal demand with infrastructure investments (as happened in China after the 2008 crisis) or with measures taken on the exchange rate of money (dollar depreciation or higher flexibility of yuan exchange rates).

Countries in surplus in the eurozone can't allow for an excessively depreciated euro because the circuit rests on the acquisition of neighboring countries' sovereign debt bonds by the same banks of central countries who, with a weak euro, would risk insolvency. On the other hand, as we saw after the subprime crisis, the circuit is only able to reproduce itself, at least in the mid-term, if the country in commercial deficit, even if it is highly unbalanced in the financial sector, actuates a kick-start policy increasing the public deficit, and certainly not decreasing it as Europe is doing. Even though it has been estimated that a depreciation of the euro would bring assets of $300 billion to the commercial balance in a short time, it isn't clear who could absorb an asset of this size. Certainly not the US, where consumers are still struggling with unburdening their families of debt, and neither can China, which can't quickly transform itself from an exporting to an importing country.

We are probably witnessing a historical process of the de-europeanization of Europe that can end in the explosion of the euro. According to some analysts, it shouldn't be excluded that, even by the end of 2010, Germany decides to leave the euro to continue with its export-oriented political economy, this time reinvesting its surplus more in Asia or Brazil than in neighboring European countries. It is a more likely scenario than a two-speed Europe with a single currency differentiated into a euro 1 (strong) and a euro 2 (weak). At stake is the survival of the European banking system and the power relationships internal to Europe and between Europe and the US. The relationship between the US and China, at least under the profile of currency exchange, is already quite precarious because there is also a weak euro in the middle of it, which forces China to devaluate the yuan to the dollar in order not to lose their market position in exportation.

Originally, the euro was conceived and created to protect Europe from the dollar and from American monetary policy. European economic and social unification wasn't possible because the Constitution was strongly centered around the unification of capital markets. It didn't adopt wages and fiscal measures between member states that would have consolidated welfare policies suitable to new processes of production and redistribution of wealth. Such coordination may have been possible with the introduction of a "european monetary snake" inside which each member state could have managed its own currency according to its own possibilities and needs. The euro, *de facto* a nationless currency, instead has worked as a vehicle for the financialization of the economy and public expenditure. It didn't reduce commercial imbalances in the eurozone, rather worsened them.

Faced with the risk of the deflation of global demand and a slowdown in internal growth, the Chinese government seems willing to increase wages and better living conditions, a strategic-political measure meant to increase its international power, not through improbable revaluations of the yuan, but through the gradual construction of a social state in a period when its European counterparts are doing everything they can to dismantle it. Since the introduction of the new labor law of January 2008, Chinese workers' wages have in fact increased over

17% and the frequency of strikes against Japanese and American multinational corporations are also on the rise. This is a process that will modify the composition of investment that has been strongly leaning, until today, toward infrastructural investments at the expense of the internal demand for consumer goods. But it is also a first sign that the US-China relationship regarding wage regulation may change, if it is true that, over the last few years, the low cost of Chinese labor and the low-cost of goods sold in American supermarkets has increased the buying power of the American worker by $1000.00 a year. It has been calculated that a 20% increase in Chinese consumption would allow a $25 billion increase in goods exported from the US, creating 200,000 US jobs. We are still far from full employment, but it is interesting to see that the global economy can be rebalanced by a new cycle of worker struggles in China.

As Silvio Andriani lucidly synthesized, "What kind of development could help us overcome the crisis? Both the hypothesis that there can be a rally of investments pulled by a revival in private consumption financed with family debt—since no one is proposing a wave of increases in redistribution—and that this increase in consumption can be pulled by the US would require reimplementing the old development model, and it is its unsustainability that brought this crisis about to start with. Even supposing that this scenario were possible, we would be laying the ground for the next crisis, which would be worse than the current one. More likely, such a hypothesis is unrealistic and the risk of a 'third depression' and the reinforcement of protectionist reactions will become quite real."

It is a veritable riddle and it wouldn't be sufficient to provide an answer invoking a quantitative increase in public demand financed through debt to counterbalance the fall in private demand caused by the first crisis. In this case, it is quite probable that the structural imbalances between countries in surplus and countries in deficit accumulated on a global scale over the past years would only get worse. This raises once more a series of questions developed in this book.

The first question concerns the interpretation of the financialization process, its progressive development beginning at the end of the '70s and its relationship to the real economy. The thesis that we have put forward is that financialization is the other side of the post-Fordist capitalism coin; it is its "adequate and perverse" form. However, it doesn't make financial capitalism less detestable. Maintaining that financialization is consubstantial to the new processes of capital accumulation means going beyond the 19th century idea that there exists a good real economy and a bad financial economy—two conflicting worlds where finance works "against" the real economy, ripping capital from its productive use, the creation of employment and wages. Certainly, the way the logic of finance works and the succession of speculative bubbles which increases private and public debt impacts the real economy, provoking closer and closer recessions. The problem is that, with financial capitalism, on a global scale, it is extremely difficult to overcome the crisis by *definancializing* the economy, i.e., reestablishing a more balanced relationship between the real and financial economy, for example by increasing investments in the industrial sector or, as in the 1930s in the US, investing in the construction of the social state.

By now, finance permeates from the beginning to the end the circulation of capital. Every productive act and every act of consumption is directly or indirectly tied to finance. Debt-credit relationships define the production and exchange of goods according to a *speculative logic*, transforming, that is, the use value of goods (theoretically all produced or to-be-produced goods) in veritable potential financial assets that generate surplus value. The demand, and the indebtedness it implies, for a financialized use value, as happened with housing during the subprime bubble, induces further increases in demand precisely in virtue of the *increase* of the price of that good. This fully contradicts the law of supply and demand typical of neoclassical theory where an increase in price reduces demand. After the ascendant phase of the economic cycle, when the inflated prices of financialized goods begin to diminish for lack of new buyers, the contradiction between debt levels (fixed in nominal terms) and prices of financial assets (which can both increase and decrease) violently explode. This triggers a selloff of financial assets in order to be able to cover the debt contracted, a selloff that in turn causes a further reduction in prices and therefore more selling (this spiral is called a debt deflation trap).

The debt crises that have characterized businesses, consumers and states for nearly 30 years are based on carry trade, i.e., borrowing at a low cost to invest in higher rendering bonds. As such, the debt crisis is, as was theorized years ago by the American economist Hyman Minsky, *inherent* and *cyclical* to financial capitalism. In the ascending phase of the cycle, in times of prosperity, businesses, consumers and states are encouraged to assume more and more risks, i.e. go into debt. Initially, such speculation is profitable and encourages more and more new subjects to go into debt in virtue of the increase in the price of financial assets. This inclusive process works as long as the capacity to repay the debt is guaranteed by new entries, but ends in flipping over into its opposite, into crisis, when the difficulty of repaying debt first begins to show, triggering a selloff of assets and an increase in interest rates.

In global financial capitalism, the margin of flexibility in interest rates used by monetary authorities is very limited. This is due to investment fluxes in state bonds, in particular in American T-bills, which lengthen the expansive phase of the debt spiral *despite* the increases in interest rates decided on by central banks in order to contain speculative bubbles. Today, more than interest rates, which are in fact, close to zero, it is the interbank market (the bulk market that banks use for their account activities) that is responsible for rationing credit to the real economy. In order to save the banking-financial system from collapse with injections of liquidity, public intervention, be it national or supranational, reveals two things: on one hand, the necessity to plug up with added demand (to prevent a crisis of overproduction) the surplus value produced in the expansive phase of the cycle through debt, on the other, to determine a process of *exclusion* from access to goods produced in the ascending phase through layoffs and the worsening of living conditions. It is during this phase that we see a selloff of excess produced goods coupled with industrial and bank capital concentrations.

Overcoming the subprime crisis caused the shift of debt from private to public sectors, but the public debt, increasing vertiginously more than anything else, is the result of the socialization of financial capital made with the taxpayer money and the creation of liquidity by monetary authorities. A kind of *communism of capital* where the state, i.e. the collectivity, caters to the needs of "financial soviets," i.e. banks, insurance companies, investment funds and hedge funds, imposing a market dictatorship over society. The "communism of capital" is the result of a historical process beginning with the recourse to retirement funds to finance the public debt of New York in the mid-seventies and, following this, the transformation of new productive processes that have changed the base of the creation of wealth and the very nature of labor.

The analysis of financialization raises a series of questions that are subject to debate. First, if it is certain that in the last 30 years profit rates have constantly increased despite frequent financial crises, it is also true that, on average, the rate of accumulation on a global scale has increased, but at decidedly lower rates in respect to profit. "Data demonstrates," Daniel Albarracin writes, "an important accumulation in Asian and developing countries, which mostly compensate for the regression seen in the US, Japan and Europe." The divergence between these two rates is surely at the origin of the coexistence of prosperity and relative growing poverty, but cannot be immediately interpreted from a historical point of view.

In our opinion, the divergence in accumulation rates between developed countries, Asian countries and new developing countries should be analyzed on the basis of the *global form* of contemporary capitalism, keeping in mind the strategic role of transnational companies that directly benefit from the high growth rates of developing countries, repatriating the surplus value realized there to invest it in financial markets, as well as keeping in mind the appearance of new political tools for coordination, intervention and supranational control, like the G20, the IMF, the World Bank, the WTO and the central banks of the main regional poles of development. The globalization of capital has internalized peripheral economies, forming the *Empire* theorized by Negri and Hardt— an empire in which the same logic of exploitation rules, even if articulated in different forms, and where the appropriation of wealth by a transnational capitalist oligarchy dominates. Today, the relationships between North and South, center and periphery are *inside* accumulation processes, every "outside" is already "inside" the process of capitalist growth.

Reasoning in terms of empire rather that imperialism (i.e., the relationship between "inside" and "outside," center and periphery, development and underdevelopment) doesn't mean underestimating the internal contradictions of global capitalism. There is no doubt that between the US, Europe, Asian countries and developing countries there are differentiated strategies regarding investment choices, monetary policy, growth stimulating measures, the role of exports and modalities of financing public debt, as we've shown in our analysis of the real tensions at play in capitalism in this period. These contradictions are, however, inscribed inside a "cooperative competition" that has the unifying objective of extending the processes of workforce exploitation and the redistribution of wealth according to appropriative logic. This does not exclude the possibility of a crisis in international relations, the beginning of a dangerous process of de-globalization based on protectionist policies and local wars to reestablish a hierarchical order of global control. The crisis we're in can have entirely contradictory and dramatic effects precisely because of its long duration and the sum of tensions that are emerging from it.

The other crucial question open to the analysis of contemporary capitalism is the interpretation of financialization beyond preconceived ideological schemes inherited from the past. There is no doubt that the separation of the rate of profit and the rate of accumulation is the consequence of policies centered around increasing stock value and transferring surplus value (dividends and interest) to investors, above all large institutional investors. This was made possible thanks to souring labor conditions, direct and indirect wage compression, precarizing labor and externalization processes of whole segments of production. That is, if the cost of labor is minimized and employment is reduced, profits increase and a part of them are invested in financial markets to guarantee financial rents. The mobility of capital, its orientation towards developing countries with high rates of profit and company delocalization are all processes that have contributed to increasing profits, without, however, triggering a new wave of general prosperity, rather an extreme polarization of incomes. We are witnessing a spiral of growth sustained by global rates of accumulation. Even industrial technological innovations, which have been considerable over the last few decades, have been applied more to compress the cost of labor and intensify the workday than to trigger cumulative growth, as was the case in the Fordist period.

According to our analysis, beginning in the '80s, the expansion of finance was the other face of extending the process of extracting and appropriating value over the entire society. Financialization and the cyclic crises that characterize it should in fact be interpreted in the light of the biopolitics of labor, i.e., the post-Fordist productive strategies in which one's entire life is put to work, when knowledges and cognitive competences of the workforce (the *general intellect* that Marx spoke about in his *Grundrisse*) assume the role played by machines in the Fordist period, incarnated in living productive bodies of cooperation, in which language, affects, emotions and relational and communication capacities all contributed to the creation of value.

In these processes externalizing the production of value, the consumer is often coproducer of goods and services, and it is in this light that financialization should be studied: as an effect of the bifurcation between the rate of profit and the rate of accumulation. The scissor process between profit increases and stagnation of investments in constant and variable capital, or rather in capital goods and wages, can be explained in terms of the transformation of the very *nature* of labor. In this gap, the extraction of surplus value, of unpaid labor, is done by capturing devices outside of the direct productive processes by using an organizational business model that draws from the productive, creative and innovative qualities of the workforce developed in extra-professional environments. The production of financial rent, with the reinvestment of profits and workers' savings (retirement funds) in the stock market rather than the creation of wage employment with investments in capital goods, has contributed to generate the increase of an effective demand necessary for the monetary realization of profits, which is to say, for the sale of goods and services holding surplus value.

On the other hand, the stagnation of real wages was in turn "compensated for" with private debt. In short, a "becoming-rent" of profits (and, in part, of wages too) came to be, a process symmetric to the production of value directly inside the sphere of the exchange of goods and services.

In our opinion, the increase in profits over the last 30 years is therefore due to a production of surplus value *with* accumulation, albeit a totally new type of accumulation because it is external to traditional productive processes. This new constant capital, unlike the (physical) machine system of Fordism, is constituted by a whole of organizational disciplinary systems (as well as information technologies) that suck surplus labor by following citizen-workers through every moment in their lives, resulting in a lengthened and densified workday (the time of living labor). These crowdsourcing strategies, leaching vital resources from the multitudes, represent the new organic composition of capital, the relationship between constant capital dispersed throughout society and variable capital as the whole of sociality, emotions, desires, relational capacities and a lot of "free labor" (unpaid labor), a quality that is despatialized as well, dispersed in the sphere of the consumption and reproduction of the forms of life, of individual and collective imaginary.

So, the American economist Robert Shiller is right when he says that in the current phase of massive unemployment, evermore a longterm unemployment, the stimulus packages shouldn't have an increase in the GDP as primary objective but rather the creation of jobs directly in sectors of high intensity labor, like education, healthcare and social services, urban infrastructure maintenance, youth employment programs, domestic aid, cultural and artistic projects and scientific research. The idea is to monetize activities that don't need particular investments in capital goods to be legitimated, activities that for the most part are already done at no cost or activities whose positive externalities, in particular in the environment, aren't immediately translated into GDP growth in the classic and obtuse cost-benefit analysis. According to Shiller, hiring one million unemployed workers in these sectors would cost $30 billion per year, or 4% of the entire American economic stimulus package, and 0.2% of the national debt.

The relationship between the apparently divergent rate of profit and rate of accumulation of the last years makes Marx's intuition, contained in his *Manuscripts of 1844*, quite contemporary: "The increasing value of the world of things continues in direct proportion to the devaluation of the world of men. Labor doesn't only produce commodities; it produces itself and the worker as a commodity—and does so in the proportion in which it produces commodities generally." The depreciation of men and women is greater the more the *production* of value is not recognized in its whole breadth, but is instead conditioned by the laws of the market (and the GDP), i.e., by criteria for measuring value tied to the relationship between the costs, direct and indirect, of wage labor and profits. Overcoming longterm unemployment must assume the evermore anthropogenic nature of the new system of accumulation; it must therefore privilege forms of labor remuneration directly tied to the reproduction of life itself. No longer the production of goods through goods, but the production of man through men.

There is something Luxemburghish about financial capitalism that, between one bubble and the next, colonizes more and more common goods. Rosa Luxemburg wrote her study on capital accumulation, where she maintained that capitalism cannot survive without "non-capitalist" economies: it is able to progress, following its own principles, as long as there are "virgin lands" open to expansion and exploitation; but as soon as it conquers them to exploit them, it takes their pre-capitalist virginity away from them and exhausts the sources of its own nourishment.

The imperialistic accumulation cycle was characterized by a precise relationship between center and periphery, development and underdevelopment. The center exported to the pre-capitalist countries of the periphery the surplus it couldn't sell internally for lack of a demand. In order to allow poor countries to import capitalist goods, the creation of external demand was based on a "debt trap," a device in virtue of which the banks of the North created the demand necessary for selling surplus through the indebtedness of importing countries. This mechanism forced peripheric countries, on one hand, to destroy the natural local economy in favor of imported capitalist goods and, on the other, to export as much of their primary materials as possible at prices determined by capitalist markets in order to be able to honor the debt. The *destructuration* of common goods, the local natural resources strategic for the capitalist development of countries in the North, had to come about *without the restructuration* of the local economy, i.e., without the possibility for poorer countries to escape poverty and their dependency on rich Northern countries, lest they suffer the same problem of selling surplus on a bigger scale. The dependency between rich and poor countries was sealed by the relationship of debt-credit.

This scheme of imperialistic relations historically went into crisis when peripheric countries matured forms of political autonomy capable of imposing autochthonous development strategies against the dependency on the predatory development of Northern countries. This is the historical result of the struggles for national liberation, struggles that transformed underdeveloped countries into new developing countries.

Today, the same historical logic of dependent relationships between the center and the periphery is found inside the capitalist empire. The central difference, between imperialism and empire, is that today "pre-capitalist" common goods are made, so to speak, by *human* primary materials, the vital capacity of producing wealth autonomously. The hidden face of financialization, of the recurrent production of "debt traps," as happened with the subprime bubble, is constituted by the production and exportation—

silent, but real—of what we call the *common*. The common is the entire knowledge, understandings, information, images, affects and social relations that are strategically subject to the production of goods. In respect to natural primary materials, which are limited, these new common cognitive and immaterial goods that capital appropriates are theoretically unlimited, hence their privatization (for example with copyrights and patents, or with the simple privatization of entire sections of public service networks) brings about the artificial creation of *scarcity* through private property.

Contemporary financial crises are moments of the redefinition of capitalist control over common goods, they produce poverty as "common poverty," moments of deconstruction-without-reconstruction of social economies based on horizontal cooperative relationships. In the crisis, the process of inclusion of common goods is overturned into a process of exclusion, which means that the access to common goods is downwardly redefined, transforming debt relations into control over forms of life, into austerity and poverty. This is the moment when wage constriction is violently manifested, exactly like the 16th century enclosures where access to land as a common good was repressed with the privatization of the land and the putting wages to the proletariat.

Today more than ever, the "pre-capitalist" nature of common goods recalls the concept of collective property against private property. "The common," writes Ugo Mattei, "has an 'ecosystem' as a model, i.e., a community of individuals or social groups interconnected through a network; in general it refutes the idea of hierarchy (as well as the idea of *competition* produced by the same logic) in favor of a *collaborative* and *participative* model that never confers power to one part of the same *whole*, putting the interest of the latter at the center of attention."

Through recurring crises, the capitalist financialization of the last few decades has upset the legal-political distinction between private property and the state. The crisis of sovereign debt, in this sense, marks the entrance of financial markets in the management of public debt, extending financial logic to the public sphere, with its rules, its privatizing discipline and the concentration of its power. This process was preceded by the privatization of public works, but with the financialization of sovereign debt it has definitively torn the ideological veil from the "counterposition" between state and market.

"The sovereign government on national territory," writes Negri, "hasn't worked for decades: to reestablish an effectiveness it uses a procedure of *governance*. But this, too, is insufficient—the same local government needs something that goes beyond a territorial state, something that substitutes the exclusive sovereignty that the nation-state otherwise possessed." The passage from government as the state modality of the regulation of growth to governance as the exercise of technocratic control—partial, punctual and local—is exactly what we have been witnessing in the international crisis of sovereign debt. It isn't by chance that the financial crisis is, *de facto*, a banking crisis, an insolvency crisis in which regional banks, from the German *Landesbanken* to the Spanish *Cajas* to nation-states and American cities, find themselves on the brink of bankruptcy, struggling to reduce their debts. It's like experiencing again the crisis of New York City in the '70s, but this time on a global scale. At that time, it was the retirement funds of public employees that saved New York from bankruptcy, inaugurating the era of the "communism of capital" and the processes of financialization that followed. Today, international financial markets are the ones that, with the "simple" differential of bond revenues, technically determine if a citizen of Greece, Illinois or Michigan has the right to retirement funds or if he or she has to resort to public assistance to survive.

This is the terrain in which austere governance and government of the common are confronting each other. The forms and objectives of the struggle "inside and against" crisis capitalism are at the same time local and global. The objectives of this struggle are clear: imposing, collectively and from the ground up, new rules to govern the market and the financial system, a social mobilization for starting anew investment policies in public services, education and welfare, the creation of public employment for the conversion of energy, a refusal to defiscalize high incomes, assert the right to wages, employment and social income and the construction of autonomous, self-determined spaces. However, the first step in constructing new alternative paradigms, new forms of common government, is totally subjective. There are no predefined recipes, there is only the challenging awareness that any future depends on us.

Appendix

WORDS IN CRISIS*

Finance has its own language and, moreover, a rather esoteric neolanguage. Many Anglo-Saxon terms are untranslatable into other languages and, above all, designate complex processes not always accessible to the uninitiated, which is to say, to almost everyone. It is thus under the shelter of this linguistic opacity that finance prospers, a situation which raises the question of democracy, that is, the possibility of publicly debating strategies, procedures, and decisions concerning the lives of all citizens. In what follows, we have selected some (not all!) words that help readers to understand the history of the most recent financialization.

---

* This brief dictionary was written on the basis of the following publications: *La grande crisi. Domande e risposte*, Il Sole 24 Ore, Milano, October 2008; Charles R. Morris, *Crack. Come siamo arrivati al collasso del mercato e cosa ci riserva il futuro*, Elliot Edizioni, Rome, 2008; Frédéric Lordon, *Jusqu'à quand? Pour en finir avec les crises financières*, Editions Raisons d'agir, Paris, 2008; Paul Krugman, *Il ritorno dell'economia della depressione e la crisi del 2008*, Garzanti, Milan, 2008.

AAA, AA, A, BBB, etc: a system (used by the rating agency Standard & Poor's) for evaluating the quality of debt assets. The more the asset is at risk, the lower the vote and the higher the earning.

ABCP (Asset-Backed Commercial Paper): a kind of unsecured promissory note (or commercial paper) guaranteed by other financial activities, particularly by securitized assets. The ABCP are generally short-term investments that mature between 80 and 180 days, issued by banks or other financial institutions in order to satisfy the need for short-term financing. These are amply employed in special purpose vehicles sponsored by the banks (see Conduit and SPV) that financed with short-term commercial paper so as to invest in long-term assets representative of the credit that was the guarantee of the ABCP. In 2007 and 2008, the value of these assets collapsed, creating a lot of problems for the financial institutions involved, who, no longer able to finance with commercial paper, had to resort to the line of credit of the sponsoring banks (that provoked a strong increase in interbank interest rates, a clear sign of banks distrusting one another).

ABS (Asset-Backed Securities): loans supplied by banks backed by income from an activity that lies immobile until maturity. But if the bank does not want to wait, it can take this activity, "wrap it up" in obligations bearing interest—"obligations guaranteed by activity"—and sell it to private funds. In such a way, the lent capital immediately returns and the bank can expand its own activity. The types of loans that most fit the issuance of ABS are real estate loans, credit for purchasing cars, insurance policies, and credit related to the use of credit cards. In sum, the ABS is an instrument of transferring credit, and the related risks, from the banking balances to third-party non-banking buyers.

ALT-A: a class of loans whose risk profile falls between so-called "prime loans" and "subprime loans." Those who take this type of loan usually have a clean personal credit history but a low capacity to produce income, conditions which allow a pronounced relationship between the value of the loan and their income.

Bailout: saving a subject close to bankruptcy by an injection of liquidity.

Basis point: a unit equal to 1/100th of a percentage point, indicating variations in interest rates, exchanges, earnings from T-bills and bonds.

Benchmark: an "objective" parameter of reference, constructed through representative signs of the risk/earning profile of the markets. It is an indication that expresses the risks related to the product of investment underwritten by a saver and is useful for evaluating the efficiency of the product of investment.

Carry trade: this instrument allows one to borrow money in countries that apply low interest rates, especially, but not only, in Japan, and to lend it in countries that apply high interest rates, such as Brazil or Russia.

CDO (Collateralized Debt Obligation): the CDO is a specific category of ABS and assets of fixed income that are not subject to regulation on the markets. Typically, the issuance of CDO starts from a "special purpose vehicle" (SVP, see securitization) that is conferred a complex portfolio of mortgage loans, residential or not, but also corporate obligations of high earning, and more still. The portfolio includes credit of various risks. The CDO is then divided into tranches or classes. The lower and the riskier one (equity tranche) absorbs the first X% of subsequent losses; the tranche (senior tranche) suffers losses only if the total losses of the portfolio exceed the quota absorbed by the lesser ones. By virtue of this protection, the senior tranche usually obtains the maximum rating (valuation), i.e., the triple A. The rating gradually decreases for the lesser tranches. The higher the rating of a tranche, the less is its earning. CDOs are very complex instruments difficult to value and are thus rather opaque. They are not homogeneous and, both at the time of issuance and successively, are traded over the counter.

CDS (Credit Default Swap): instruments of a larger family of credit derivatives that allow the transferring of the credit risks relative to a determined financial activity from a subject intending to purchase a guarantee against risk to a subject willing to lend it. The Credit Default Swap is similar to an insurance policy. CDS are traded over the counter, i.e., on the parallel markets where contracts and modalities of buying and selling are not standardized and not tied to a series of norms (admission, control, informative obligations, etc) governing official markets.

Collateral: an asset pledged by an agent who owns a debt.

Conduit: the conduit is also known as special purpose vehicle. It has to do with a corporate entity created for a specific purpose, usually by a financial institution. For instance, if a bank wants to securitize a series of real estate loans, it confers these loans on a "special purpose vehicle" created on purpose and, on this basis of activity, the new company issues securitized assets. It is essential that these conduits be not formally tied to the parent company; otherwise, they would be recognized as an integral part of the group and their balances would have to be consolidated, thus impeding the transfer of the risk and the dispersal of requirements of capital. This separation decreases at the moment when (like in 2007–08–09) the bank is in liquidity crisis and is dependent on a sponsoring bank to receive credit.

Credit crunch: a contraction (restriction) of credit supply from the banks following a financial crisis in which they are particularly implicated. It is used to "cool down" inflation. The constraint of credit thus occurs on the wave of bank failures.

Deleveraging: when investors, who entrusted themselves to high-risk financial instruments—managed by institutions of the so-called shadow banking system—withdraw or threaten to withdraw their money from the markets and the system becomes susceptible to a cycle that is auto-reinforced by a forced liquidation of assets (deleveraging), a process that further increases unpredictability and reduces the prices in an entire series of asset categories.

Derivatives: financial contracts stipulated between two contractors whose value depends on the trend in the underlying activity. Underlying activities can be financial (shares, obligations, interest and exchange rates, stock market indexes) or real (as raw materials).

Fair value: literally estimate, fair price; the term was introduced by the accounting principles IFRS (International Financial Reporting Standard). It is a method of valuation based on the presupposition that values in balance reflect "real" values. At times, however, a fair value valuation becomes difficult for some activities, particularly the immaterial activities and some financial activities lacking exchange market.

Hedge fund: these are non-regulated funds that operate in accordance with "short selling," i.e., selling assets betting on a reduction of the market (operations of norm not allowed to other typologies of funds), or, vice versa, to "go long," i.e., speculating on an increase in assets. The assets of hedge funds can be invested in any type of activity permitted by regulation, thus assuming short-term positions or departing from all prudential norms of containment and the division of risk. The objective of these funds is to attain the highest earning between those granted by the market without any preclusion with regard to both the areas of investment and the type of financial instrument. They make extensive use of derivatives.

Interbank rate: the interbank market is meant to provide for short-term cash imbalances where those who have excessive funds lend them to those who need them. Each morning 50 main European banks must share the interest rates they intend to use in the debit/credit operations with the other banks (inter-bank rate). During the crisis of trust between the banks that broke out with the discovery of the abyss of toxic assets, the interbank rate increased considerably.

LBO (Leveraged Buyout): an operation of acquiring a company with the use of a high financial leverage. The debt owned by the (acquiring) company X, generally obtained by granting concessions on guaranteed shares or property of the (acquired) company Y, is then generally repaid either with cash flows generated by the acquired company or by selling branches of the acquired company (so-called non-strategic business unit).

Leverage: the faculty of controlling a high amount of financial resources through the possession of a small part of such resources, and thus with a low use of capital. For the banks, having caused leverage meant issuing derivative financial instruments with ever-more complex structures.

Libor (London Interbank Offered Rate): the rate of interbank market in London. The Euribor is its European equivalent. These two rates serve as reference for all the other interest rates.

Liquidity (cash): liquidity designates the treasury of an agent; the capacity that offers a market to sell its assets "easily," thus the capacity to cease being assets and become cash.

Mark-to-market: an application of the criterion of fair value to accounting: which is to say, of evaluating the activities at the root of market prices rather than historical cost (the cost at which they were purchased). With a view to establishing the "truth of balances" and rendering them transparent, the accounting norms usually call for using "mark-to-market" to evaluate the financial activity and passivity. With respect to the advantages of reliability and transparency, the mark-to-market criterion can aggravate the unpredictability of shares, with pro-cyclical effects, in periods of strong increases or strong drops of prices on financial instruments.

MBS (Mortgage-Backed Securities): a version of ABS obtained by securitization of real estate credit.

Monoline: insurers of bonds.

Non-banking financial system: "The structure of the financial system changed fundamentally during the boom, with dramatic growth in the share of assets outside the traditional banking system. This non-bank financial system grew to be very large, particularly in the money and funding markets. In early 2007, asset-backed commercial paper conduits, in structured investment vehicles, in auction-rate preferred securities, tender option bonds and variable rate demand notes, had a combined asset size of roughly $2.2 trillion. [...] The scale of long-term risky and relatively illiquid assets financed by very short-term liabilities made many of the vehicles and institutions in this parallel financial system vulnerable to a classic type of run, but without the protections such as deposit insurance that the banking system has in place to reduce such risks" (Timothy Geithner, United States Secretary of the Treasury, a speech delivered at The Economic Club of New York, June 2008).

Panic: "Sometimes," writes Krugman, "panic is simply panic: an irrational reaction on the part of investors that is not justified by the actual situation." In such cases, those who remain lucid are rewarded for not losing their head. "In economics, however, the kind of panic that—whatever the motive that gives rise to it— autojustifies itself is much more important. The classic example is that of rushing to cash machines: when those in rush try to withdraw all their savings at the same time, the bank must sell its goods at lowest prices, going bankrupt as a consequence; those who do not allow themselves to be seized by panic are worse off than those who effectively lost their head."

Price/earning ratio or P/E: index given by the relationship between the quotation of a stock price and earning per share. If, for instance, the price/ earning ratio of a share equals 15, the stock pays 15 x for generated earnings (example: with a P/E of 15 and a share price of $1, we have an earning rate of 6.7%).

Private equity: investment on the part of specialized subjects in quoted and non-quoted companies. The operator of private equity is a subject financing small companies with good prospects of development, with the intention to make them grow and then demobilize its shareholding at higher prices.

Rating agency: an agency specialized in valuation (notation) of the credit risk of an issuer of obligations, that is, of structured obligations guaranteed by a plurality of mortgage loans. The main agencies are Moody's, Standard & Poor's, Fitch, and DBRS, all American.

Ratio: a relation, indicator resulting from comparison of two quantities, for instance the profit of a company and its assets.

ROE (Return On Equity): the earnings from net assets. It indicates the profitability of their own means, that is, those made available by shareholders of a company (such as a bank).

Securitization: consists of the transformation (giving way to a "special purpose vehicle" or SVP that has as its exclusive objective the realization of such operations) of credit, or also of future cash flows, into an asset. Example: let us suppose that the bank has a number of real estate loans among its activities; the bank can decide to securitize them, i.e., to issue securities that have these loans as the guarantee. These securities are then sold to private or institutional investors and the bank thus returns the money to the lenders: the funds that the bank obtains can be used to expand its own activity. The securitized assets, like normal obligations, have a maturity date and an interest rate, and the debt service is tied to refunds and payments of interest on the part of the original debtors. The bank, besides having the advantage of mobilizing activities of little liquidity, also diminishes the risk tied to those loans: the risk is passed on to the investors. The government, on a state or local level, can securitize as well.

SPV (Special Purpose Vehicle): see Conduit.

Subprime: in American language, subprime are real estate loans of lesser quality offered to subjects with high risk of insolvency: with previous episodes of insolvency, with low or even uncertain incomes, lacking other forms of wealth.

Swap: an agreement between two parties who decide to periodically exchange incoming or outgoing cash flows in accordance with preestablished conditions.

Systemic risk: a situation in which a local failure triggers a series of other failures with the threat of global collapse of the financial system.

Toxic asset: "toxic" financial assets are comprised of irrecoverable credit "contaminating" banking balances and, consequently, creditor companies. The "toxic assets" can also end up in the portfolios of savers. Once they would have been defined as "waste paper" or garbage.

ACKNOWLEDGMENTS

The first version of this text was published in a book edited by Andrea Fumagalli and Sandro Mezzandra, *Crisis in the Global Economy, Financial Markets, Social Struggles, and New Political Scenarios* (Semiotext(e), 2010). I thank Gianfranco Morosato, director of Ombre Corte, and the coauthors of the volume for having me write and republish, in a rather revised and updated form, this essay. I also thank my colleagues at the social research center with Dipartimento di Scienze Aziendali e Sociali della Scuola Universitaria Professionale della Svizzera Italiana (SUPSI) for having discussed the version that is published here. In particular, I thank the colleagues Spartaco Greppi and Federico Corboud for helping me to deepen a lot of questions related to financialization, offering their competence, their time, and their friendship. A personal acknowledgment goes to Fabio Casagrande, Matteo Terzaghi, and Silvano Toppi for encouraging me to publish this work in a short period of time.